People are excite
autobiography

~

A DELIGHTFUL CHRONICLE OF AN ORDINARY MAN WHO FOUND A DEEP AND PERSONAL RELATIONSHIP WITH AN EXTRAORDINARY GOD!

My dear friend, Martin, illustrates the life of one who surrenders to Christ, and then finds Him to be a true Friend and Strong Tower in the dark valleys and the mountaintop experiences in life. You will be challenged and inspired as you walk with Martin in his search for *Truth, Freedom, Faith, and Love.*

Don Showalter,
President, Hearts Alive!

"A GREAT DEMONSTRATION OF GOD'S POWER: TAKING THE OCCURRENCES OF ONE'S LIFE AND MAKING GOOD!"

In his book, *If I Had Only Known,* Mart describes how adversity and setbacks, *(enough to swallow any man in sorrow, defeat and despair),* were given back to a compassionate God, who used them powerfully in his life for good. I laughed! I cried! In the end, I saw a prototype image of how I want to live my own life.

Paul Kurtz
Owner, Hemisphere Coffee Roasters

HARD WORK, DEEP FAITH, AND A PERSEVERING SPIRIT!

That's the secret to the peaceful, victorious life Martin lives today. *If I Had Only Known* will both inspire and challenge you to become a Christ-loving overcomer that loves life!

John Schmitt
Common Ground Ministries

"SPIRITUAL, EMOTIONAL, and FULL OF TRUTH!"

Growing up Amish, I can totally relate to the way Martin was raised. His journey to freedom is one that I, myself, took 36 years ago. This book is a bold illustration of the grace of God in a man's life. You'll be inspired to treasure every day that you're given."

Dave Weaver
Ordained Evangelist

"A LARGE TREE HAS GOOD ROOTS!"

"Reading through each chapter of Mart's life story, I began to see and understand, more and more, the roots of his tree. The strict religious background didn't always make sense, but it was a crucial part of his work ethic and influenced his life.

"HIS ROOTS, GROWTH, AND LEARNING JOURNEY MAY NOT BE ALL THAT DIFFEERENT THAN YOURS."

Seeing how Mart faced life challenges and came through each one, I was inspired to grow in my own life and faith. I am better for having known him.

Dan Utz
Friend

If I Had Only Known

An Amish Man's Search for Truth, Freedom, Faith, and Love

Martin Graber

GW Publishing
Sarasota, Florida

If I Had Only Known - *An Amish Man's Search for Truth, Freedom, Faith, and Love*
Copyright 2022 by Martin Graber
ISBN # 978-1-387-86970-1

GW Publishing
Sarasota, Florida

Under the covering of:
Christian Leadership Institute
Sarasota, Florida

Cover Design by *GW Publishing*

Cover photo purchased from *Shutterstock*

Internal Design by Mary Ann Manzo

Editing by Bernice Ditchfield

To purchase additional copies, go to **www.lulu.com**

Printed in the United States of America

Foreword

Let me start off by saying... Everyone comes into this world in the same way - as a child. We don't get to choose our parents or our date of birth. The Bible tells us that God created our world and all that is in it for His purpose and glory.

We are to be His reflection
to all of creation.

In Acts 17, we find the record of the Apostle Paul, on Mars Hill, confronting the philosophers of his day. His proclamation is clear: Mankind comes from one blood; we are all God's offspring; we're created in His image, and it's God who gives each of us life and breath.

Martin Graber is a good friend of mine. We've known each other a long time, and I can't express enough how proud I am of him for putting his life story in writing. Page after page, his transparency reveals the purity of his heart in wanting to please God. It also reveals that the foundation of his faith in God is strong, strong enough to withstand the many misunderstandings that come in serving Christ.

Most of all, it is this very foundation, that
God has built in Martin, that highlights a path
for others to discover God in the same way.

As the offspring of God, we've been given the freedom of choice. *"Choice"* means the right to choose, created by God, and accountable to God. The origin of sin and death came as a *wrong* choice made by Adam and Eve. We in turn are their offspring, and are born with their sin nature.

If I Had Only Known is God's
Plan of Redemption depicted through
the life of Martin Graber.

According to John 3:16, God sent His Son, Jesus Christ, that we all might be saved. The Bible makes it clear that Jesus is the only way one can escape eternal death. The way to salvation is not through a manmade religion; it's not by good works; it's by grace, and grace alone, through a God-ordained faith in Jesus Christ, who said, *"I am the way, the truth, and the life, and no one comes to the Father but through Me."* That said, I exhort you to read Acts 17 and the book of Colossians.

I first met Martin and Carol in 2006 while I was ministering at Sunrise Chapel. They invited me for dinner one evening and we've had a sweet friendship ever since. I have a lot of respect for Martin's zeal for the things of God, and his deep desire for his people to receive Jesus as their LORD and Savior.

I, too, grew up as an Amish boy in Ohio and can relate to many of his stories. There's a lot that I appreciate about the Amish culture, the family, and the church family, which is very close. The Amish have good work ethics and a desire to let their lifestyle be a witness for God.

If I Had Only Known is Martin's life story -
the good times and the hard times.

It's about learning how to get up after being knocked down again and again. It's in the midst of all these ups and downs that Martin discovers God in a very real way. He realizes God has a plan for his life and yields to that plan.

Of course, no one is perfect. Everyone makes mistakes, but life is so much more than mistakes made. Martin learns from them, works through them, and overcomes them.

***If I Had Only Known* reveals how to
become an overcomer through a
personal relationship with God.**

As you open the pages of this book and begin to read, I want to
challenge you to do something. Invite God to speak to you through
Martin's story, then look for God in your own life story. More
than anything, God wants to make Himself known to you in a
personal way. He wants a relationship with you.

***If I Had Only Known* is evidence that
the mysteries of God are not hidden
<u>from</u> you, they're hidden <u>for</u> you!**

Rev. Reuben Beachy
Christian Leadership Institute

A Note from the Author

I worked all my life and I never took the time to really share with people what was on my heart. Now that I'm 83, I'd like to show the LORD how thankful I am for His abundant blessings.

**If it wasn't for Him, nothing
would have been possible.**

Now that I'm retired, I'd like to help people. I'd like to inspire them. I wonder, *"Is there some piece of wisdom that I can leave behind that will make someone's life a little better?"*

**Maybe the story of my life is the answer -
where God took me from, how He protected me,
how He made Himself known to me, and how He
filled my life with love and blessing in abundance.**

My hope is that people will realize that God is in everything we do. I spent my entire life in the business of making cabinets. Believe it or not, that's exactly where God found me, and my life has never been the same since.

We only have one life to live here on earth. It's my prayer that God's magnificent light has somehow touched others through me. Perhaps He'll touch you through my story.

To God be the Glory,

Martin

*"Though your beginning was small,
Yet your latter end would increase abundantly."
Job 8:7*

Table of Contents

CHAPTER 1

Farm

Birth

I was born September 25, 1939 in Fort Wayne, Indiana to Harvey and Margaret Graber. I was their second child, and their firstborn son, which I later discovered had its privileges. They named me Martin.

My father and mother were good parents. Dad worked hard, and so did Mom. There's one thing, however, that sticks out in my mind.

> **Over all the years, I don't ever remember hearing my mom and dad say *"I love you,"* to each other, or to us kids, for that matter. Even so, our home was filled with love, all the same.**

It was no one's fault, that's just how it was in those days. People weren't so outwardly affectionate the way they are today. They were private, but very committed when it came to marriage, raising a family, and the Amish Church.

The Farm

We didn't have a lot of money growing up. Some may say we were poor, but we didn't think of ourselves that way. Dad put all he had into the purchase of the farm. That's right, I lived on a farm. Who can complain about that? Certainly not me! After all, there were ponies and horses in the barn, and I'd ride them without saddles and bridles. What's better than that?

> **As a boy, I imagined I was in the wild, wild west. Oh, how I loved playing cowboys and Indians!**

Farm life is a great learning environment for children. It taught me a lot of things, especially how to provide for myself. Surely, you've seen television programs about surviving in the wilderness? Back in those childhood days, an Amish boy growing up on a farm was some of the best training around for just such a thing. In the Amish lifestyle, everything is learned from scratch. There's no assistance from the modern world of technology, so in the end, you grow up being self-sufficient in the direst of situations. Personally, I think that's a good thing!

> *"Aspire to lead a quiet life, to mind your own business,*
> *and to work with your own hands, as we commanded you,*
> *that you may walk properly toward those who are*
> *outside and that you may lack nothing."*
> *1 Thessalonians 4:11-12 NKJV*

Chores

Farm life is by no means easy. It's work, work, and more work, especially in the Amish community. There were eight of us Graber kids in all, and every one of us had chores to do. When I was six or seven years old, I milked the cows, morning and night. It was normal for us kids to get up at 5:30 in the morning to take care of our chores before going to school. Aside from milking the cows, we slopped the hogs, fed the chickens, tended to our pets, you name it. And the girls were by no means exempt. They helped outside the house as well as inside. Mom would have them canning the harvest, making soap, mending clothes, and so much more.

Back in the day, all the heavy work on the farm was done by horses.

By the time I was ten years old, I was harnessing up the horses on my own, hitching them up to the equipment, and driving them in the fields.

That's how we got the plowing and disking done. My main job was to get the fields ready for planting. The soil had to be prepared in advance, then Dad would come along behind with a horse-drawn planter to do all the actual planting of the crops. In addition to all that, we did all our own harvesting and butchering, not to mention all the maintenance, painting, and handyman work that needed to be done.

Rarely did you get a day off. There was always something that needed tending to - making hay, harvesting the grain, hauling manure, farm-stuff! Even when it rained, there were things to do in the barn.

Animals

There were always horses on the farm. Some were pets, but most were used strictly for work. We used them to pull loads. I'll tell you a secret I learned at a very young age: You have to build relationships with the animals if you want to get them to do what you want them to do. Otherwise, they can make the simplest of tasks difficult.

My pet horse was a Tennessee Walker named Skipper. He was a riding horse, and I did a lot of riding!

> **Whenever I'd call to Skipper out in the field,
> he'd see me and come running right to me.**

Sometimes, I'd ride my horse in the field or down the road to the neighbors. Other times, I'd ride beside the nearby railroad tracks. I loved riding! It gave me a sense of adventure and freedom - just me and my horse. Of course, there was the daily upkeep of the horses - brushing, feeding, cleaning the stalls, and so forth. That's a given.

We also had dogs and cats on the farm - too many to count. Our main dog was Shep, and as his name implies, he was a German shepherd. Whenever we were bringing in the animals from the field, Shep would go with us. He was a master at rounding them all up.

Of course, there were hogs, chickens, and rabbits, not to mention all the ducks and geese. Those ducks and geese were so noisy - worse than a dog! Every time someone drove up the path, they'd start cackling away. Dad raised several hundred of them at a time.

Farm life was work, but as kids we enjoyed it. That was our life. We didn't know anything else. There was no money for worldly entertainment, and the Amish Church didn't allow such things anyway.

**We simply made the best of what each day
brought our way. That's farm life for you!**

Challenges

As with anything, there are always challenges, and farm life is no exception. As a boy, I took note that most of these challenges were due to the beliefs of the Amish Church that ruled over us.

For example, my Grandpa Schwartz pastored an Amish Church that labeled motors as *"worldly and sinful,"* so whenever we visited him, we helped him out by hand pumping the water into a big water tank that his cattle drank from.

My dad was always a bit progressive and forward thinking. That said, when he married my mom, they moved out of Grandpa Schwartz's district, (where you couldn't use a motor), to a community that allowed power from windmills. Certainly, that made a man's work a little bit easier.

Bath Time

Working hard means getting dirty and sweaty. I have to say that bathing, in those days, was not what it is today. For starters, it was done right in the kitchen by the stove where it was warm. Mom would fill up the galvanized tub with water that was heated in the stove, and then we'd all get in line and wait our turn to wash up. Of course, the girls and boys bathed at separate times. The girls always went first, and the boys ended up with the dirty water. Regardless, the process was the same. When it was your turn, you stepped in the tub, washed yourself quickly, got out, and dried off. Then the next person in line would jump in, and so on.

Have you ever heard the saying, *"Don't throw the baby out with the bath water?"* That's because the baby was usually the last one to be bathed in the tub before the water was thrown out! Really, the baby was washed in a dishpan, not a bathtub, but now you understand the meaning behind that old saying.

The Family Table

Probably one of the greatest things about growing up on a farm was *"The Family Table."* Every day, the family sat down for our meals together - breakfast, lunch, and dinner. Mom spent most of her time in the kitchen, and much of it cooking! Just about every morning, she'd prepare a full breakfast of bacon, ham, eggs, and fried mush made from cornmeal. There's an old song I used to sing as a boy...

> *"Cornbread and buttermilk*
> *are a country boy's delight!*
> *I eat them every morning,*
> *at noon, and at night.*
> *Some people like fried chicken,*
> *and others like the ham,*
> *But cornbread and buttermilk.*
> *makes me who I am!"*

In addition to all of Mom's home-cooking, I really looked forward to the conversation around the table. First, we always prayed before our meals. My dad used to say, *"If you can't thank God for what you eat before you eat it, then you're no different than the animals."*

As we ate, we'd share with one another what we did all day, the people we ran into, and what was on our mind - those sorts of things. In the early days, there were only five or six of us around the table for supper, but as I got older, my other siblings came along. By that time, I was out of the house.

"When I think of my dad, I'm reminded of coffee on a Sunday morning before church, and a spoonful of vanilla ice cream any time of day!"

~ Marlene O'Donovan, daughter

"It's no secret that Grandpa has a great sense of humor and a love for ice cream. We've all heard his famous words... 'After a meal, you always need some ice cream to fill in the cracks.'"

~ Hannah Eicher, granddaughter

"Grandpa is a man who loves nothing above God, his wife, his children, grands and great-grands... and ice cream, of course!"

~ Caleb Quaintance, grandson

A Sweet Treat!

If there's one sweet treat that has followed me throughout my lifetime, it's ice cream, and oh, how I love it! You have to understand something. We were poor! During the winter months, we'd take the ice that froze over in the pond, put it in the freezer, and use it to make this delicious treat. With free ice and cows in the barn, we were never without it! That said, I'm pretty sure I've eaten ice cream every week of my life.

Back then, all the ice cream was made by hand in a bucket. Mom would put all the ingredients together, and since I was the oldest boy, it was my job to crank the handle. The more I churned the cream, the firmer the ice cream got, and the harder it was to crank. My little brother, Enos, would have to sit on the bucket to keep it from moving around, while I kept turning the handle. After an hour or so, the ice cream was done. That night we'd have it for dessert, and if there was any left over, we'd put it in the ice box outside, for the next day.

Farm Boy Forever!

There's an old saying...

> **"You can take the farm boy off the farm, but
> you can never take the farm out of the farm boy."**

When I grew up and got married, I bought my own farm. (You'll hear more about that later.) Even today though, at eighty-three years old, you can catch me riding with my boy on the big farm equipment - combines and tractors. It never gets old. Oh, those machines are too big for me now. I hate to admit it, but I don't like to do the driving anymore, so I let my son do it. Just try, though, and keep me off one of them. Not a chance! It's in my blood. And if I'm not in there with him, I'm following him around the field in my John Deere Gator.

Everything Has Its Time

Ecclesiastes 3:1-8

"To everything there is a season,
A time for every purpose under heaven:

A time to be born, and a time to die;
A time to plant, and a time to pluck
what is planted;

A time to kill, and a time to heal;
A time to break down, and a time to build up;

A time to weep, and a time to laugh;
A time to mourn, and a time to dance;

A time to cast away stones, and a time
to gather stones;
A time to embrace, and a time to refrain
from embracing;

A time to gain, and a time to lose;
A time to keep, and a time to throw away;

A time to tear, and a time to sew;
A time to keep silence, and a time to speak;

A time to love, and a time to hate;
A time of war, and a time of peace."

CHAPTER 2

Family

Mom

My mom, Margaret Schwartz Graber, was a good mother - very loving and caring. In the Amish world, the mother is the hub of the home. While Dad was out working the farm, Mom ran the house. Everything in our home was hand-made, pretty much by Mom herself. What we harvested, she canned. Sewing, quilting, making soap and candles, not to mention tending to all of the household chores and cooking, Mom did it all!

Now mind you, Mom was no pushover. You had to listen and do what she told you to do, or she'd get the broomstick out and hit you with it. She'd say sternly, *"When your dad gets home, I'll let him deal with you!"* That was the last thing any of us wanted, so we minded our manners with Mom.

One thing I look back on fondly about Mom is when she and her sisters would sing. *Wow!* They were really good singers and harmonized beautifully. For the most part, they would sing German songs and hymns. In the wintertime, when family and friends would get together, the homemade wine and popcorn would get passed around, the men would play checkers, and the people would have a sing-along.

Back then, homemade wine was a common drink. Dad would make two fifty-gallon kegs for just such an occasion.

A few people might get a little tipsy and loose-tongued, here and there, but for the most part it was just a fun time for all! Of course, the little kids didn't get any wine. You had to be in your early teens to indulge. Instead, we all drank homemade lemonade, and oh, how we loved it - so sweet and refreshing!

Dad

Harvey Graber may have been a farmer, but his workload went far beyond working in the fields. Whatever needed to be done, Dad did it. He also helped others in the community with big projects that couldn't be done alone, like putting up homes and painting barns. The Amish are really good at working together to accomplish such things. They're not afraid of hard work. As a young man, my dad even helped build State Road 37.

Together Time

Living in the country, Dad would occasionally have to make the ten-mile drive into Fort Wayne to do the shopping and as the oldest son, I was the one that got to go with him. Boy, did I love that time with my father. Not only that, but there was always the chance that he'd get me a hot dog, ice cream cone, or root beer from *Coney Dogs.* Now that was a real treat!

To get to Fort Wayne, we often rode with our neighbor, Andy Berch. Dad wasn't allowed to drive because it was against the Amish rules for the Amish to own and drive cars or trucks. Andy wasn't Amish, so he could drive.

Sometimes, our neighbor would be driving into town, and we'd just ride along with him. Other times, Dad would hire the neighbor to drive us. To the Amish mindset, that was considered acceptable.

I think I had a good relationship with my dad. Later in life, when I owned my own business, Dad used to come to my shop, sit in the office, and watch what was going on. He was content doing that.

The Demise of the Lazyback

I mentioned earlier that Dad had a little progressive streak in him. In those days, the fact that he owned a *lazyback* on his buggy was considered by some to be excessive. Most Amish buggies came with a simple bench seat. A lazyback, on the other hand, was a seat back that you could lean back against as you drove.

Mom was more conservative. She grew up in a community where her father was a pastor of a church that said seatbacks were sinful and unlawful. One day when Dad was out doing an errand, Mom took it upon herself to retrieve a saw from the barn and cut that seat back right off their buggy. When Dad came home, boy was he mad! There was no way to fix what she'd done. When all was said and done with, Mom admitted that she did it to appease the judging people of her father's congregation.

If there was one issue of discord in my parents' marriage, it certainly centered around the nonsensical ways of the Amish Church. Dad wanted to live one way, but Mom pushed back.

Just a Taste!

Back in Dad's early years, before he married my mother, Dad actually owned his own car, and took it on a road trip to Canada. That said, he certainly had a taste of the goodness of progress. Years later, after he'd settled down, Dad wanted to get a tractor. Surely, that would be a great asset on the farm, but mom frowned upon it. In the end, he did purchase one, but how he utilized it day-to-day had significant restrictions. He was only allowed to use it for belt power to run the thrash machine.

Amish rules forbid a man to actually get on the tractor, ride it, and work the land with it.

Rule Breakers are Shunned!

When members of the Amish Church break the Amish rules, the entire community shuns them. That means no one is allowed to have anything to do with them anymore. The Amish don't fellowship or do business with them. They won't sit down at the table and eat with them. Basically, they disown them and keep their distance from them.

One time, there were some families that left the Amish Church in our district and went to a nearby conservative church that allowed *lazybacks*. Not long after, their progressive mindset expanded to include the use of automobiles. These families all ended up being shunned by our community for doing such a terrible thing. Dad, however, refused to ever shun any of them. He didn't think it was right.

**Dad may have pushed things to the line,
but he himself never stepped over the line.
All his life, he remained a part of the Amish Church.**

Later in life, an opportunity presented itself in which Dad could have made a move that would transition him from the Amish Church to a less restrictive Amish-Mennonite church. Even so, Dad knew Mom was set in her ways and decided not to.

Two Wonderful Grandfathers

Grandpa Schwartz, my mom's father, was one of the pastors of a local Amish Church. He was highly respected by many in the community, and very special to me. As a boy, I always sensed Grandpa Schwartz was a sincere man who took a genuine interest in me and wanted to spend time with me. Every time Grandpa would visit, he'd give me a coin. He didn't do that with all my brothers and sisters, just me, probably because I was the oldest son. I kept those coins in a little cup in the cupboard, and from time to time, I would check to make sure the pennies were still there. As a young lad, I thought I was rich!

Grandpa Graber, my dad's father, was very different. I loved him, too, but for other reasons. Growing up, it was no secret that Grandpa Graber lost everything in the Great Depression. That's why my father started his family from scratch - there simply was nothing to inherit. Even so, my family, along with all my aunts, uncles, and cousins would always gather together at Grandpa Graber's house during the holidays for a time of food, fellowship, and fun. To be honest, it wasn't actually Grandpa Graber's house, though that's how we referred to it. It was Uncle Levi's house. Grandma and Grandpa lived with Uncle Levi.

For all the time I knew Grandpa Graber, he was never able to work. He had a gallstone and someone was always caring for him. As a boy, I'd go and stay overnight, from time to time, to help keep him company. Grandpa always got a kick out of telling us kids ghost stories - that was his thing.

Christmas

Christmas day was always a time of celebration, yet simple. That was partly because we didn't have a lot of money, partly because it was in the *olden days,* and partly because we were Amish. There was no extravagance - no Christmas trees, stockings, ornaments, wreaths, or ribbons. Most certainly, there was no Santa Claus or big gift exchanges.

Regardless, our family always looked forward to breakfast on Christmas morning. Next to each place at the table, Mom would set a special holiday treat. We never got toys. It was always something to eat like a candy bar or an orange. Sometimes it would even be wrapped up.

**We didn't know any different. As simple as
all this sounds, Christmas was a day of blessing!**

I do recall that when I got older, there was a gift. I vaguely remember getting a pair of roller skates one year, but the emphasis was never on the gift-giving or receiving. Instead, we focused on family and being together.

Our big Christmas celebration was an all-day event, held on an appointed day between Christmas and New Year's. That's when the extended family would all head out to Grandma and Grandpa Graber's for a carry-in dinner. The women would prepare the food in advance. Pork, chicken, and beef dishes, along with vegetables, home-made bread and pies were all set out on the table, buffet style. Looking back, there had to be over a hundred of us celebrating together in this holiday gathering!

Christmas wasn't a religious time, at least not for me.

To be fair, the church and family may have been talking about Jesus' birth, but if they were, it was in German, and I never made that connection. There was one thing, however, that you could always count on. There would be plenty of singing - mostly hymns, and always in German. We sang a lot of Christmas songs too! The women, in particular, did a lot of the singing - always acapella, no instruments.

I always enjoyed getting together with all the cousins at Christmas. The older boys would go rabbit hunting, and they'd use us little guys to chase the rabbits out from their hiding spots, in the tall grass and bushes.

During the winter months, we would often ride in bobsleds when we went to visit our aunts and uncles for meals. As children, we would hook our sleds behind the bobsled and enjoy the ride. Oh, how fun that was!

Butchering was also done in the winter time. I remember one year we butchered eight hogs! Generally speaking, if guests arrived unexpectedly for a visit, it wasn't unusual to butcher a few chickens on the spot, prepare and cook them, and serve them for supper that very night. That's how it's done on the farm.

My Siblings

Altogether, there were eight kids in our family. From oldest to youngest was Verna, myself, Enos, Esther, Leah, Louie, Davie, and Harvey.

Growing up, I was close with my sister Verna and my brother Enos. We went to school together on the same bus, and we all played together. Sometimes at night, Verna would read to us.

We all slept in one room upstairs. There was no stove up there to keep us warm, just a register in the floor. Oh, how we hoped the heat would rise up and give us some warmth during the night! From time to time, I'd stand over the register trying to warm up, only to be pushed off by my brother or sister. It was a bit of a game we played, I suppose. Looking back, the windows were so bad, that sometimes the snow would blow through the cracks. That said, we wore long johns to bed for pajamas. Thank God for Mom's homemade quilts!

Being the oldest, Verna was always looking out for me. In the same way, I looked out for my younger brother, Enos, who was always attempting to tag-along with me.

I'll never forget the time Enos got hurt. I was doing my chores, hauling manure out in the field, and Enos wanted to sit with me on the spreader, for a little ride. I thought that would be okay, but when we hit a little bump, Enos fell off. The horse ran over his leg and broke it bad. I always felt that was my fault. I should have been more responsible in caring for him.

All Boy!

All said and done, I was born a little Amish boy, ornery as could be. I used to take pleasure in teasing my younger siblings and making them cry. I guess I was pretty aggressive in a lot of things. I made a lot of trouble for my dad, and I got a lot of whoopings, which I have to admit I deserved.

As a kid, I didn't like being Amish. For one thing, the church elders didn't want us speaking English, so we were taught to speak German in the home and in the community. I remember one time, asking my mother, *"Why can't we just be like other people?"*

"Be still!" she responded, meaning *"Be quiet!"*

After that, there was no further discussion of such things. That's what it was like in those days. There was no arguing or debating with your elders. If you did, they ignored you or reprimanded you.

CHAPTER 3

Childhood

Public School

When I was six, I started first grade at the local public school. It didn't take me long to discover that I wasn't like the other kids. For one thing, they all spoke English, and I, of course, spoke German. That meant that I had to learn their language - a language I was not allowed to speak at home, so there was no reinforcement.

Of course, I made friends, but the non-Amish kids made fun of me all the time. They'd call me *Long-haired Dutchman* and other dirty names, but through it all, I managed to do well in school. I was on the honor roll from fourth grade through eighth. Learning came easy for me, because I loved to read. History was my favorite subject. I liked learning about important things that happened in the past.

Our school had a little library that our class would often go to. Keep in mind, it wasn't like the huge libraries you see today with floor to ceiling bookshelves, tables, comfy chairs, and displays. Oh no!

> **Our school library was nothing more than a small room, but oh, how I loved to go there!**

I would get so excited hunting for the books I loved most. My favorites were Jim Hinkle's stories about dogs, and of course I could never turn down an adventure in the wild west! By the time I left school, I had pretty much read every book in that place!

I admit the library books weren't that thick, plus I was a fast reader. It didn't take me long to read through a book, cover to cover.

You have to understand something - books were my television.

As I read page after page, I would visualize the story in my mind, and before long, I'd be caught up in the adventure of it all. It was near impossible for me to put the book down until the story came to its end. How I wish I could still read like that today!

After our library visit, we'd all go back to the classroom for more teaching. I never could seem to wait until I got home to start reading my new books. More often than not, I'd put my newest library book inside my school book and read while the teacher was teaching. I was still listening, but I certainly wasn't giving the teacher my undivided attention. One time, I got caught and was told to stand in the corner. I didn't like being singled-out like that, but looking back now, I deserved it. I should have been paying better attention to the teacher.

Overall, I really enjoyed going to school. Even so, I only attended through the eighth grade. After that, I went to work on my dad's farm. That's just how it was.

I Almost Died!

I didn't know it, but I was born with a belly button that never closed up correctly at birth. One day while playing basketball at school, someone threw the ball to me and it hit me straight in my belly. Later that night, we went to my uncle's house for supper, but I was so sick that I just stayed outside and laid my head down on the buggy seat. I never told my parents anything.

The next morning, as I lay in bed sick and delirious, Verna saw that something wasn't right with me. Immediately, she told my mom and my parents brought me to the hospital right away. The doctors ended up operating on me and removed my navel.

One day, during my recovery, I overheard some visitors say that they didn't think I was going to pull through. For sure, I thought I was going to die. In those days, the doctors gave you ether, before your operation, to put you out. That alone would make anyone sick. For days after, I was so nauseous, I couldn't eat a thing. Even so, my mom stayed by my bedside the entire time. Before long, I got better and went home.

Church

Growing up in the Amish Church, I knew about God, but we weren't really taught anything from the Bible about Jesus. As a family, we attended an Amish Church service every two weeks. The meeting place was simple. We sat on benches - the men on one side and the women on the other. Children under twelve sat with their parents.

As a young boy, I couldn't wait until the service was over. More than anything, I wanted to get outside in the open air. To be honest, I wasn't interested in religion. That's because the sermons were all spoken in German, and I didn't understand what was being said. In addition to all that, the people all spoke in different dialects.

As children, we were taught at home to speak German, but we were never taught how to read it, so I never really got a good handle on the language. Then when I went to school, I was expected to speak in English. You can see how the whole thing could be a bit confusing.

When I got older, I stayed outside with the other boys during the service. We all hung around the horse stable and just talked with one another.

The Bible

Growing up in an Amish home, I saw my parents read the Bible. From time to time, my mom would even read a Bible story to us kids. We were never taught or encouraged as children, however, to read the Bible ourselves - that is until Uncle Levi came around.

One winter season, Uncle Levi started an Amish Bible school for kids in our community. That's where we learned to sing Amish songs, and how to read German. Uncle Levi taught us.

Community Bible School

The Bible school was open to all the young people in the neighborhood, and there were close to twenty from the Amish community who attended. At 14, I was one of the youngest. Uncle Levi was a bishop and taught from house to house. Bible school was wonderful, but it didn't last long.

> **When our parents and Church elders discovered Uncle Levi was teaching things the Mennonite Church embraced, they didn't approve of it.**

The Mennonites were known for being less rigid in their rules. Their ways were looked down upon and rejected by the Amish Church. Uncle Levi's descent from the strict Amish ways truly did create an uproar. That said, the Bible study stopped and Uncle Levi moved to Michigan. By this time, Grandpa Graber had passed away, so Grandma Graber went to Michigan with him.

Intrigued

Who understands all that kind of stuff when you're a kid, right? Personally, I loved visiting Uncle Levi. One time, when I was eleven or twelve, I discovered that Uncle Levi kept a couple of guitars in his shack out back. They were kept out there, because it was forbidden in the Amish community to actually play musical instruments.

> **That shack housed a number of interesting things from Uncle Levi's youth - a time before he was married.**

To me, the highlight of it all was that guitar of his!

Somehow, I mustered up the courage to ask Uncle Levi if I could have that guitar, and to my surprise, he said yes! Oh, how excited I was to take that guitar home with me. I couldn't wait to learn it. I also knew that I couldn't let my parents see me with it. They would never allow such a thing, so I hid it under the back seat of the buggy and covered it up. Unfortunately, Mom found it and that was the end of that. She destroyed it. To my disappointment, I never did get the chance to make music with it. Over the years, Uncle Levi and I have never forgotten that story. Uncle Levi lived a good, long life. He must have been close to 92 when he died.

A Secret Hiding Place

Needless to say, there were a few things I managed to get away with in my youth. One thing in particular was a handheld radio I purchased when I was fourteen. I knew it didn't coincide with Amish rules and that my parents would never allow it, so I hid it upstairs, in a little crook in the wall, behind a board.

There was a ventilator between the joist and the ceiling, and a board was placed in a way that allowed the heat to go up into that room. One day, I knocked the board out, and attached a fastener to it, so the board could be turned. It was the perfect space in the ceiling for me to hide such things - my own secret hiding place.

In those days, I thought I was *King of the Road!* After all, I had a radio. No other Amish guy had a radio, no sir! For the most part, I only took that radio out to use it when no one else was around, and I'd listen with excitement to the *Grand Ole Opry!* Oh, how I loved that country music! Imagine having to sneak around just to listen to music, but that's what you had to do. On occasion, I'd invite my friends over and we'd go somewhere secluded with that radio and listen together. They loved it, too! Afterwards, no one ever said anything.

Disillusioned

The older I got, the more disillusioned I became with the Amish Church. There was no God-connection, just a lot of man-made rules that differed from one region to another. To me, the rules and rituals made no common sense, and the hypocrisy of it all had a strange, suffocating effect on me.

For example, if you had a nearby job, you could do the carpentry work, but you had to get yourself there. If you had a horse and buggy, you could drive that, but driving a car or having someone pick you up with a car was forbidden. If by chance, however, someone happened to be driving by and offered you a ride in their car, you could accept, as long as it wasn't pre-arranged.

Now where's the common sense in that? And to top it all off, the Amish believe that the person driving the car will one day end up in hell because of it. Meanwhile, of course, they are all going to heaven for being good rule-followers. Not to mention, that the Amish community in the next county who have different rules, well... they'll go to heaven too, despite the fact their rules are not the same.

Amish Godliness

Understand this, the Amish are a very religious people, but not in the way you think. It's not because they follow the Bible or the Law of Moses. No! They make up their own laws, and as I said, those laws differ from one Amish community to the next.

The Amish believe that by adhering to the rules of the Amish Church, they are made righteous - or right with God. I believe that they sincerely want to be righteous, but they just don't know how. Certainly salvation doesn't hang on whether or not you drove a truck to the marketplace, right?

By abstaining from certain activities and the world's technological advances, the Amish people convince themselves they are all the better for it, before God.

In addition, they believe that by staying true to their manmade laws, they will be accepted by God. Now you won't find that in the Bible, but it's the foundation of their religious ways.

I don't believe the Amish Church was always like that. I've been told that things changed when WW1 broke out, and people became fearful.

Instead of trusting God and following the teachings of the Bible, the Amish locked themselves into a culture of legalism.

They decided, *"We won't change with the world, because the world isn't a safe place to live."* Many put their faith in God aside, and put together random rules and restrictions to keep them safe from the chaos around them. In time, the Amish Church came to believe that if you don't follow those rules you're doomed.

What the Bible does say:

"There is none righteous, no, not one."
Romans 3:10

"For all have sinned and fall short of the glory of God."
Romans 3:23

*"For the wages of sin is death, but the gift of
God is eternal life in Christ Jesus our Lord".*
Romans 6:23

*"But God demonstrates His own love toward us,
in that while we were still sinners, Christ died for us."*
Romans 5:8

*"...that I might be found in Him, not having
my own righteousness which is from the law,
but that which is through faith in Christ,
the righteousness which is from God by faith;"*
Philippians 3:9

*"For by grace you have been saved thorough faith,
and that not of yourselves; it is the gift of God,
not of works, lest anyone should boast."*
Ephesians 2:8-9

*"...that if you confess with your mouth the Lord Jesus,
and believe in your heart that God has raised Him
from the dead, you will be saved.
For with the heart one believes unto righteousness,
and with the mouth confession is made unto salvation."*
Romans 10, 9-10

CHAPTER 4

Free

Leaving Home

Farm life was great, and my family was wonderful! Growing up, my home was a place of peace, and I knew I was loved. Even so, it seemed the older I got, the more unsatisfied I became. More than anything, I wanted to get out. I needed to get out! Let me be clear about something...

> **It wasn't my family or the farm life that drove me away. It was the Amish rules and their hypocrisy. It was suffocating me, and more than anything I was determined to shake it.**

That said, as soon as I turned sixteen, I left home. I didn't tell my parents in advance that I was going. I just made arrangements for my friend Jonas to pick me up, and that was it. Of course, it didn't take long for my folks to discover where I was staying, and they desperately wanted me to return. We sat down and I listened to everything they had to say, but in the end, I didn't go back.

> **Knowing Dad, I have to wonder if there was a little part of him that understood where I was coming from and why I had to go.**

Regardless, when our conversation ended that day, I felt Dad's only reason for wanting me to come home was because he needed help on the farm. That wasn't a good enough reason for me to stay.

Sometime later, I discovered that the Amish Church punished my parents for my leaving. I was labeled an *"ungeihorsome"* child by the church elders who saw me as wayward, unteachable, and untamable. Because of that, my parents were excommunicated.

Free at Last!

Living with Jonas, I was finally free! When I wasn't working, one of the things I loved to do most was play music. I got myself a guitar and mandolin and taught myself how to play. Later, I learned the banjo and harmonica. Even today, at eighty-three years of age, I'm learning the fiddle. For sure, I was born to make music. It's something that has always brought great joy to my soul!

Rumspringa

Perhaps there are a few things that don't quite make sense to you. Understanding Rumspringa might help fill in some of those gaps. The term *"Rumspringa"* means running around, or living a loose, immoral life. Some people refer to it as *"sowing one's wild oats."* It's an Amish thing that starts around age sixteen and goes until you decide to become a member of the Amish Church.

Young people have the freedom to live unhindered, according to their fleshly nature, before settling down.

They go out partying, drinking, and dancing, not to mention, they sleep around. It's nothing out of the ordinary for a young man to walk a girl home at night, after a date, and proceed to sleep over that evening in the girl's bed. The parents just go along with it, because that's how they themselves were brought up. If a girl gets pregnant, Rumspringa is over. The young man marries the girl, they settle down, and they raise a family together.

Now I know you may think of the Amish as religious, but they certainly aren't religious about living a pure life before God. If they are religious about anything, it's about following their man-made laws. With Rumspringa, there is no Biblical, moral code, for the Bible says in *1 Timothy 4:12...*

*"Let no one despise your youth, but be an example
to the believers in word, in conduct, in love,
in spirit, in faith, in purity."*

As with anything, it's important to understand that not all Amish go along with Rumspringa, though most do. Those who call themselves Christians and who follow the teachings of the Bible would most certainly put their foot down to such a practice.

**So why do so many embrace Rumspringa?
Basically, the Amish claim that each person
joins the Amish Church of their own free will.**

No one is forced to live an Amish lifestyle. That's true, though some parents are more pressuring than others. Rumspringa, thereby, is everyone's opportunity to test whether or not the Amish way of living is better than living in the world.

"Keep yourself pure."
1 Timothy 5:22

The Sweetheart of My Youth

My roommate, Jonas, had a sister named Marjorie. I knew Marjorie, because she was from the same Amish community as me. Growing up we attended the same church and the same school. She was a year behind me.

As teenagers, all us kids would gather together on Sundays after church and hang out together. Marjorie and I were both part of that group. She was fourteen and I was fifteen. I wasn't much into Rumspringa, but Marjorie was a little.

When I was seventeen, I was working hard, playing my music, and totally into cars. Dating wasn't a priority on my list, but a friend of Marjorie's was persistent in convincing me that I needed to take Marjorie on a date. Finally, I gave in and asked her out.

Marjorie was very pretty, and we had a really nice time together. We liked a lot of the same things - hillbilly music and square dancing - so of course, I wanted to get to know her better. Once we started dating, it didn't take long for me to ask her to go steady and she said yes. As time went on, we fell in love.

Time To Settle Down

One day, Marjorie told me she was pregnant. After talking about it, we decided that we wanted to do something so we could be together officially and lawfully. That said, we picked a date, March 4, 1958, put on our best clothes, and went into the city to see the Justice of the Peace. It was just the two of us that day, but unforgettable all the same. Afterwards, we went out and got something to eat. We were young, in love, and quite excited about being married and starting a family together.

> *"He who finds a wife finds a good thing,*
> *and obtains favor from the LORD."*
> *Proverbs 18:22*

An Unexpected Twist

A few weeks later, Marjorie and I went to see her parents to tell them what we'd done. They were not happy, to say the least, and they certainly didn't approve of us not getting married in the Amish Church.

To them, we weren't legally married, and her dad thought it only right for me to take measures to correct that. I agreed.

So, I went back to the Amish Church for Marjorie. I certainly loved her, and at the time there didn't seem to be any other options.

CHAPTER 5

Married

Following Church

Right up front, we had a little problem. The fact that I had never been water baptized was a major issue with Marjorie's parents. You see, there are two pre-requisites to getting married in the Amish Church. First, you must be water baptized, and second, you must become an official church member. Before I could do either of those things, I had to complete an eight-week instruction class called *"Following Church."*

Once I agreed to go through the course, Marjorie and I moved into her parent's house. During that time, there were four families, (no children), all under one roof, and living on the farm. Prior to Marj and I getting married, her brother Jonas, (my former roommate), had also gone back to the Amish Church in order to marry his girlfriend. He and his wife were living there, too, so I was by no means friendless. During the day, I worked at a boat factory, and whenever I could, I helped out on the farm.

Confused!

It didn't take long for the haunting effects of Amish hypocrisy to renew its grip on me. That's because the whole *Following Church* course was taught in German, which I still didn't have a good handle on. Clearly put, I didn't understand most of what they were saying. In addition to that, the rules themselves still didn't make sense. Looking back now, it seems to me they pulled a bunch of Bible verses out of context in order to justify their Amish ways.

**I admit I didn't understand the fullness of what
I was agreeing to, but I went along with it anyway.**

The Wedding Day

Upon completion of the *Following Church* course, everything was made official during a Sunday morning church service.

**I confessed my faith in the Amish Church,
agreed to follow their rules, was water baptized
by sprinkling, and then they married us.**

The marriage ceremony was simple. We wore our Sunday best and said our vows before the congregation. Afterwards, Marj's family had a big supper for us at their home. About a hundred and fifty people came and celebrated with us. Someone even made us a beautiful wedding cake. The next day, I went to work.

Married Young

Marjorie and I were pretty young when we got married. She was eighteen, and I was nineteen. I always thought getting married young was a very good thing for me. As I focused on my wife and worked hard to make a living for our family, I was left with little to no time to get involved in things that could take me down the wrong road.

Purchasing the Farm

We were only a couple years married, when Marjorie's father died rather unexpectedly. Soon after, I purchased the family farm outright, and Marjorie's mom lived with us. The farm became our home - the place where we would raise all of our children. It's still in our family today.

My Queen

Marjorie turned out to be a queen... my queen! She was beautiful, loving, always positive, and dedicated to me and the children. Whenever we would have a gathering of sorts, Marjorie was the life of the party!

**Truly, she was the sweetheart of my youth,
a wonderful wife, the mother of our children,
and the one who ran the home while I was at work.**

I always say, *"Treat your wife like a queen and she'll treat you like a king."* We had a very happy life together.

Proverbs 31:10 says it best...

"...a virtuous wife - her worth is far above rubies."
Proverbs 31:10

"Growing up, we all had our chores to do. Us girls all helped Mom get things done around the house - doing the dishes, cleaning, and gardening.

With 10 kids, she was a busy mom!

When we were really young, Mom used to do all our hair for the weekend. One at a time, each of us girls took our turn up on the chair and Mom would braid it. When one was done, she would call the next and the next, until everyone's hair was perfect!"

~ Rebecca Schwartz, daughter

"When I think of my dad, I envision his strong work-worn hands, busy making something beautiful out of wood, and I smell sweat and sawdust from a hard day's work."

~ Marlene O'Donovan, daughter

"Dad has a work ethic that makes his grown adult children tired!"

~ Marlin Graber, son

"Dad found fulfillment in working hard for his family. We never lacked for anything! I'm grateful for the work ethic he instilled in me."

~ Wilma Zehr, daughter

"Dad has always been a hard worker, and he instilled that value in each of his children."

~ Rose Eicher, daughter

"My dad always prioritized providing for our family. Over the years, he taught me what it means to work hard, and I'm thankful for him and his example."

~ Lynn Graber, son

"Grandpa's amazing work ethic has set an example for all of us grandkids."

~ Celina Jones, granddaughter

CHAPTER 6

Work

A Strong Work Ethic

I don't recall a time in my life when I wasn't working. As I mentioned earlier, growing up on the farm, there were always chores to do, and all us kids took part from a very young age. By the time I was a teenager, those chores grew into full-time farm work. Hard work was just part of life, and I loved it!

Surely, that's where the seeds of a strong work ethic were planted in me. The Amish are hard workers!

When I was 19, I went to work in the engineering department of a local boat company. Of course, building boats is a whole different thing from building cabinets, but that was my initial foot in the door of artistry. It was a very good experience and I learned a lot there.

From there, I went to *Grabill Cabinets* where I learned the basic skill of cabinet-making. I started out in the assembly area and worked my tail off. Somehow, cabinet making brought out the creative side of me. I loved figuring out how to bring a project to completion. I put in a lot of hours, but I didn't mind because I loved what I was doing.

After several months, I was promoted to supervisor over the assembly area I worked in, as well as the stain room. That move allowed me to learn the manufacturing side of things as well as the painting.

I realized early on that it was to my advantage to learn as much as I could, so I stepped into every opportunity that brought growth.

A Mentor

The first kitchen I ever did was for a man named Amos Zehr. Amos was a prominent businessman, one of the biggest developers in Fort Wayne, and a friend of my mom and dad. He and his son, Joe, developed subdivisions and sold lots.

Amos saw potential in me and took a liking to me, so he offered to set me up in business for myself making cabinets. His proposal was very generous. He would back me financially by putting up a building for me and furnishing the capital necessary for me to get started.

As great as that all sounds, I didn't take Amos up on his offer. To be honest, his proposal scared the daylights out of me! I wasn't ready to take the leap of faith Amos was offering. I lacked the confidence necessary to do such a thing and felt I still had a lot to learn.

Not long after, Amos was the one who helped me get all the permits and everything I needed to establish my own cabinet making business when the time was right.

Working with Furman

Instead, I went to work with Marjorie's cousin, Furman Steury. I knew Furman from way back in my teenage years. Back then, I worked for him laying block and brick. When he heard what Amos was offering me, he came to see me.

At the time, Furman was building 15-20 houses a year and they all needed cabinets. Furman knew I was doing cabinetry and asked me to come work with him, so for two years, that's what I did. It was an easy decision for me to make, because I had my job, I had cabinets to make, and I knew I was going to get paid.

Looking back now, that's when I developed my skills at cabinet making, and came to understand the cabinet-making business.

I was living the American dream!
I worked hard and took pride in what I did.

Then one day, Furman told me our company was getting too big to continue operating the way we were. The time had come to incorporate, so we could officially and successfully move ahead.

"PERSEVERENCE... That's the word that comes to mind when I think of my father. He has this steadfastness about him. It's a continual effort to do or achieve something despite difficulties, failure, or opposition."

~ Wilma Zehr, daughter

The Forming of a Partnership

In 1969 *Dutch Made Cabinets, Inc.* was officially established, though our clients simply referred to us as *"Dutch Made Cabinetry."*

There were three equal partners - Meredith Yoder, Furman Steury, and myself. From the beginning, Meredith focused on sales. Furman was building twenty homes a year and had all the orders. Of course, those homes all needed kitchen cabinets and I was the cabinet builder. We were in business!

It just so happened that a friend of my dad, Andrew Berch, heard about what I was doing in business and generously offered to loan me and my partners the money we needed. His offer is what allowed me to be an equal business partner. Not only that, he gave us such a low rate on the loan, that we ended up building two buildings instead of one.

"And my God shall supply all your need
according to His riches in glory by Christ Jesus."
Philippians 4:19

"When I was a young boy, my family lived on a connecting
farm, and I was forever crossing over the fence to get to
Uncle Mart's house. Uncle Mart was always at work in
the cabinet shop, which at the time was in his home. Later,
it became Dutch Made, the amazing cabinet factory which
he built just down the road."

~ Jonas Steury, nephew

As kids, we didn't see Dad a lot. He was a very busy man.
When he came home at night, he was tired, and we all had
our chores to do. Dad put in a lot of hours, often working
long after the employees went home. It wasn't unusual for
us kids to help him out at the shop. One time when I was six
or seven years old, Dad laid out all the packages of cabinet
hinges and knobs on the counter, and us kids opened them all
up and set them out for the workers to use the following day."

~ Rebecca Schwartz, daughter

"Growing up, I mowed Grandpa's grass and helped him
around the house with his MANY projects. When I got a
little older, I started working in his shop doing maintenance.
In time, I worked my way up to the drafting department."

~ Dr. Darrin Schwartz, grandson

"Grandpa taught me how to work hard and
to always put God and family first!"

~ Trent Eicher, grandson

The Desire of My Heart

I loved making cabinets! At the time, my work was my life. Even so, believe it or not...

Work was where I first awakened to the Presence and Goodness of God!

From the very beginning, I had always wanted to do something that my kids could help me with. You know... have a shop where they could come and work with me. It says in the Bible that the LORD will give you the desires of your heart if it's of pure motive, and that's exactly what the LORD did with me!

"Delight yourself also in the LORD,
And He shall give you the desires of your heart."
Psalm 37:4

Establishing a business was a lot of hard work, day after day, month after month, and year after year. Oh, how the time flew by! Then one day, ten years in, I was crossing the railroad tracks when it suddenly hit me...

The Good LORD had given me the very desire of my heart, and I had never truly thanked Him for it!

Over the years, pretty much everyone in my family had come through the shop. There was always a job opening! Some passed through, others stayed on for years. There were different kinds of jobs, from cabinet making to office administration, so there was literally something for everyone!

In my mind, it wasn't just a job, or a paycheck. My kids, my grandkids, and eventually the great-grands were in a good environment where they themselves could develop good character and a strong work ethic. Oh, how it blessed my heart to be able to provide that for them, as well as having them around me!

Right then and there, as I drove along, I began to thank the LORD for His goodness to me. Songs of praise flowed from my mouth and great joy filled my soul! Surely, the Presence of the LORD surrounded me that day!

A Shift in Thinking

That day my philosophy of life significantly changed. When I recognized that God had given me what I asked for, I suddenly became keenly aware that God was not merely influencing my life, He was in control of my life - full control!

It seemed He had a plan for me and that He was navigating me through it, keeping me on course.

"'For I know the plans I have for you', says the LORD,
'plans to prosper you and not to harm you,
plans to give you hope and a future.'"
Jeremiah 29:11 NIV

"Martin's a smart businessman, humble. He'll tell you, "It's not me, it's the LORD," and He's quick to mentor young people. He himself was never afraid to go to other successful businessmen for advice. If something goes wrong, Martin sees the bigger picture and says, 'It's gonna be okay. We're going to fix this!'"

~ Hank Byler, friend

Mentorship

I also saw that I was in a position where I could be an example to other people, influencing them to do the right things, so I yielded to that.

For example, one time an employee of mine made a huge mistake that really annoyed me. I was so irritated by the whole thing, that I chewed him out real good! When the whole ordeal was done and over with, I returned to my office and closed the door. Of course, I didn't feel good about my response to what happened. Not long after, a young man, who just happened to overhear the whole thing, came to my office and confronted me privately about my outrage.

"Martin," he said. *"What you did was wrong! You need to apologize to that guy."*

It was in that moment that I realized the people around me were watching me, continually taking note of what I did and said.

I woke up to the understanding that my attitude and life speaks to people, and I knew I needed to be responsible for that. So, before the day was over, I went to the man and apologized. I told him I was sorry for how I handled the situation. From that point on, I was much more conscious of what I did and said.

As time went on, I also determined in my heart to be a man of my word. When it came to my customers, dealers, and such, I saw the value of keeping my promises. If I told them something would be completed by a certain date, I made sure it was, even if we all had to work into the wee hours of the night to get it done. As a Christian, I knew the importance of operating in integrity so as to glorify God - not just in my home, but in my business. For that matter, in all areas of my life.

"Martin Graber is a man of his word."

~ Liz Firebaugh, CKD
Author of Design with Taste

Tithing

Not only was I a mentor, I knew it was important to have a mentor. Amos Zehr was a true gift from heaven. I was young and new in the cabinet making profession, and Amos was a much-needed advisor who shed light and wisdom on my business endeavors. Amos was also a godly man who taught me about *Tithing* and *Kingdom Giving*. I'd never heard of tithing before. It wasn't something the Amish Church taught, but Amos brought me right to the Bible and pointed out this scripture found in the book of Malachi.

> *"'Bring all the tithes into the storehouse that there may be food in My house. And try Me now in this,'* says the LORD of hosts, *'If I will not open for you the windows of heaven and pour out for you such a blessing that there will not be room enough to receive it.'"*
> *Malachi 3:10*

Tithing is about giving 10% of your income back to God. I know that some might think, *"Why would you want to do that?"* but God has done so much for me, I'm glad to follow this Biblical instruction that brings blessing. Not only that, Amos talked me into making a kitchen, disassembling it, taking it to Haiti, and installing it in a hospital there. What a rewarding experience that was!

The truth of the matter is this:
No matter what I gave to God, He always
seemed to bless me back many times over.

> *"Give and it will be given to you: good measure, pressed down, shaken together, and running over will be put into your bosom. For the same measure that you use, it will be measured back to you."*
> *Luke 6:38*

Break Away!

Business may have been booming, but there was still one, major, underlying problem:

The false virtue of the Amish lifestyle continued to weigh heavy upon me, and for the longest time, I felt like a caged animal.

At twenty-seven years of age, I owned my own company and not long after, I quit the Amish Church for good. I have to say, they made it easy for me. Amidst all the success, it didn't take long for the elders of the church to begin badgering me about the evil worldliness of *Dutch Made Cabinetry*.

One of the Amish rules said that you could only have six feet of cabinets in your home, and by no means could you have a sink in your kitchen. People had to get their water outside and transfer it to a dishpan in the kitchen, so they could wash their dishes after a meal. The kitchen cabinetry I was producing didn't reflect that way. Because I refused to alter or quit my business, the Amish Church basically kicked me out.

Shunned

I still owned and lived on the farm, so I was still part of the local community, but the people were instructed by the church elders to shun me. People were told not to have anything to do with me, and they weren't allowed to work for me. In addition to all that, I was removed rather quickly from all invitation lists regarding community events. From that point on, my family and friends refused to sit down and eat with me - even my sister Verna and my brother Enos. Needless to say, there were no more big family gatherings for Marjorie and me.

By this time, my dad had passed away, but mom was still alive. I still visited her, but even she shunned me. She'd let me in the house, and she'd prepare food for Marjorie and I, but she wouldn't eat with us. Conversation was at a minimum and strained at that. I can still hear her saying, *"I just wish you wouldn't be in the world."*

I explained to my mom, *"We are not of the world. We live in it, but we are not of the world."* I showed her the scriptures in the Bible that supported my stand and she listened. After that, she never said much about it.

As far as being rejected goes, I felt it was their loss, not mine. I have no regrets leaving the Amish Church. If anything, I'm mad at myself for not convincing Marjorie to break away with me at the very start of our marriage. I shouldn't have folded to her parent's pressures to get married in the Amish Church.

**As a young man, I allowed myself to be bound
by their religious laws that didn't make sense
when I could have been free.**

Searching

When I left the Amish, I didn't know nothing. Looking back, I was an aggressive guy trying to figure out what life was all about. I made a lot of mistakes... but for God. Truly, I was on a search... a search for Truth, Freedom, Faith, and Love.

Jesus said,
*"I am the way, the truth, and the life.
No one comes to the Father except through Me."*

*"And you shall know the truth,
and the truth shall make you free."*

John 14:6 and 8:32

CHAPTER 7

Happy

"Here is what I have seen: It is good and fitting
for one to eat and drink, and to enjoy the good of all
his labor in which he toils under the sun all the days
of his life which God gives him; for it is his heritage.
Ecclesiastes 5:18

Family Fun

For a while there, Marj was having one baby after another, tending to them, and running the house. All the while, I was at work building my business, so I could feed them! We both put in long hours. That said, of course we looked forward to family time, weekend getaways, and annual vacations!

Generally speaking, the Amish are what you would call *home-bodies.* Vacationing and going outside one's community for a little family fun was considered worldly and frowned upon. Marj and I found this Amish mindset to be both stifling and ridiculous. We talked about it at length and chalked it up to Amish hypocrisy. At some point, we made the decision not follow such rules. We never snuck around. We just did what we did, and that was it.

The Lake

One of the places we would bring the children from time to time was Lake James. Marj would pack up the picnic basket and coolers with sandwiches and snacks, we'd bring along blankets and chairs, and somehow, it all came together and made for a wonderful afternoon. Lake James had a little beach with boats. The kids were easy to please - they just splashed around and swam in the water all day. Oh, how they loved that!

"Our cousins lived next door to us, so we always played together. Every night in the summer, we'd be by the fence, and they'd come over to play crochet in the yard with us."

~ Rebecca Schwartz, daughter

"During our Amish days, Dad and Mom would hire a driver to take us to the lake on Sundays. I loved the picnic lunches Mom would pack, along with swimming in the water. Up until I was 10 or 12, I don't think us kids knew anything about that kind of life. The Amish would certainly consider such an adventure worldly."

~ Mel Graber, son

"When we were little, Dad made a bobsled - a square, covered box, fixed on runners, and pulled by horses. In those days, the snow stuck to the roads, making it just right for sledding. Before leaving to go to Grandpa and Grandma Graber's, Dad would hook a couple of sleds behind the bobsled and we'd each take turns riding on them along the way. It was so much fun!"

~ Rebecca Schwartz, daughter

"I don't remember Dad being around a lot in my younger years when he was starting up his business, but what I do remember are the camping trips we took to bluegrass festivals. That's where I saw the love of music in him."

~ Rose Eicher, daughter

Camping and Bluegrass

When it came to weekend getaways, Marj and I loved to go camping. We'd plan out our getaways in advance, hoping to find a campsite where there was a bluegrass festival going on. That was always fun. Our good friends, Richard and Clara Miller or Jerry and Margaret Wicky would often come camping with us. That always made our time around the campfire more like a concert. Marj had a great voice and would often sing along.

"So I commended enjoyment, because a man has nothing better under the sun than to eat, drink, and be merry, for this will remain with him in his labor all the days of his life which God gives him under the sun."
King Solomon, Ecclesiastes 8:15

"Our family has always enjoyed music. Dad and Mom would load us up in the motor home and take us to these bluegrass music festivals where we would camp out and listen to different bands play and sing."

~ Mel Graber, son

"Mom was a great organizer. Whenever we went camping, she would get as much as possible done in advance as she could, so she wouldn't have to work so hard during the trip. From packing up our clothes to preparing snacks, she had the routine down pat. She'd have all the food cleaned, prepped, and stored in gallon bags, so we had plenty snacks, and never had to stop along the way for food."

~ Rebecca Schwartz, daughter

Florida

We loved the opportunity to get away from the daily grind, the cold Indiana winter, and just have some fun. Florida was the perfect getaway!

I first came to Florida when I was 16-years old. I suppose you could say, I got sand in my shoes and could never get it out! Oh, how I loved the beach! Really, I loved everything about Florida!

About a year or so after Marj and I got married, we came to Florida for the first time, and brought along with us our first child, Wilma. Our friends Pete and Mary Ann Zehr came along, too, and brought their little baby, Lester, with them. Together, we all stayed in a little house in *Pinecraft* - an Amish/Mennonite community in Sarasota. We stayed a couple weeks and had a wonderful time. Years later, who would have guessed that those two little babies, Wilma and Lester, would end up getting married?

Pretty much every year after that, Marj and I, along with our growing family, returned to Sarasota for a couple weeks of relaxation and family fun. Eventually, we rented a condo on Siesta Key so we could be close to the beach, and of course, we did all the family-friendly Florida attractions like *Disney* and *Cypress Gardens* as well. This became our home away from home for the generations to come!

> *"Growing up, our family took many trips to Florida where we grew to love the sandy beaches and the warm weather. Today, we bring our own children there."*
>
> ~ *Rose Eicher, daughter*

CHAPTER 8

Faith

A New Church Brings New Life

Although my membership with the Amish Church was revoked, Marjorie continued to attend with her mom. After a while, I suppose I got tired of sitting at home by myself, so I found another church, *The King Church*, and began attending regularly. Marjorie was fine with that, and sometimes the kids would come with me.

The King Church was Amish-Mennonite. King was a pastor whose church had broken away from the traditional Amish Church, so they weren't so restrictive. Best of all, the preaching and teaching of Bible studies were all done in English! It was a good move for me, and I grew in my faith in leaps and bounds.

> *"When Dad left the Amish Church, I remember he started digging into God's Word. I can still see him laying on the floor reading his Bible."*
>
> ~ *Rebecca Schwartz, daughter*
>
> *"I was 16 when we left the Amish, and I remember the change in Dad after he found Jesus. It was an amazing transformation!"*
>
> ~ *Wilma Zehr, daughter*
>
> *"Over the years, my father's life has changed in many ways, but the one thing that has always remained steadfast and true is that he is a righteous man with extraordinary faith, trust, and obedience to the will of God."*
>
> ~*Marjorie Vetter, daughter*

"When I think of my dad, I hear bluegrass music echoing throughout our house."

~ Marlene O'Donovan, daughter

"When Dad first took lessons on the banjo, he would practice early in the morning. I'd hear clickety-click, click, click, and think, 'Oh no! Not again! It's so early!'"

~ Rebecca Schwartz, daughter

"I'm totally blessed that my father raised us kids up on good ole, bluegrass, gospel music! Today, my husband and I carry on that same tradition with our son, Isaac. Whenever Dad is in town, he comes and jams with our bluegrass band. Growing up, the banjo seemed to be Dad's instrument of choice. These days, it's the fiddle!"

~ Margaret Schwartz, daughter

"Having Grandpa play with us in the band is just fun! I didn't even know that he played the banjo, so it was a really cool experience having him teach me a few licks. Moments like that are ones I will never forget!"

~ Isaac Schwartz, grandson

"Grandpa has always loved to play his banjo and sing. We all admire this talent!"
~Jaeden Lengacher, grandson

"Dad loved having people to the house. Almost every weekend, someone would be at our house playing music."

~ Rebecca Schwartz, daughter

Brothers in the Faith

While I was at *King Church*, I met Richard Miller who would become a longtime friend. We both had a love for music. We couldn't play instruments in church, that wasn't allowed, but our families would go camping together, and we'd play gospel and bluegrass music around the campfire. It was always a wonderful time. We both played the guitar, and I also played the banjo. Later, Richard came and worked for me at *Dutch Made Cabinetry* for about thirty years.

We had another friend, Jerry Wicky, who was from another church. He also played music with us. Often, it was the three of us. Jerry played the fiddle. Now that I think of it, he played pretty much everything. Richard would often record us playing together. Sometimes, Marjorie would sing with us.

When the three of us weren't jamming on our instruments, we often talked about scripture. In those days, we lived and breathed God's Word. We were good for one another that way. We didn't just talk about the Bible, we walked it out in our daily lives.

Unity

For two years, Marjorie and I attended two different churches. Then one day, Marjorie made the decision to leave the Amish Church and join me and the kids at *King Church*. What a joy it was to worship God as a family in spirit and in truth. Marjorie and I enjoyed the services and Bible studies, while the kids all attended Sunday School.

Of course, when Marjorie left the Amish Church, it was her turn to be shunned. Her mother, who was born on the farm, had grown up there, and had lived there with us for the past twenty years, made the decision to go live with one of her other children and their family.

As challenging as that was, the blessing we experienced worshipping God in unity, as a family, far surpassed that.

As much as the *King Church* was a blessing, I didn't realize at the time that it was only the first stepping stone towards freedom. We stayed there a handful of years, but as I got involved more and more with music, I was asked to leave. The *King Church* didn't engage in the use of musical instruments.

"I was about twelve years old when our family left the Amish Church. When the decision was made, we all understood it was a change for the better. As a boy, I just knew it was a good thing, and I wouldn't want to ever go back! When the shunning happened, I just saw that as hypocritical! Unfortunately, it's still done in the Amish community today."

~ Marlin Graber, son

"When Mom and Dad left the Amish Church, it was hard for me, because our cousins and friends weren't allowed to play with us anymore. I remember my mom telling me to take off the black Amish bonnet or she'd burn it. 'At some point you have to let it go!' she said.

The good side of it all was that our family started going to Sunday School and Summer Bible School. We'd never done anything like that in the Amish Church, and those things were interesting to me. I was so eager to learn! Today, I'm glad Dad made that decision. It changed my life for the better."

~Rebecca Schwartz, daughter

Growing a Business and a Family

Owning a business requires a lot of determination and dedication for it to succeed. Plain and simple, it's a lot of work, and I loved it! While I put in sixteen-hour days at the office, Marjorie ran the household and took care of the kids. All in all, we had ten wonderful children, four boys and six girls.

**Wilma, Melvin, Marlin, Rebecca *(Becky)*,
Margaret, Rose, Martin Jr. *(Marty)*,
Marjorie *(Marj)*, Marlene, and Lynn.**

I really enjoyed having a family, being a father, and a husband. When the kids got older, they all came and helped me in the shop. As I said, that was one of the great desires of my heart - having my children work with me. Not only that, for the most part...

**My children grew up outside the Amish Church.
They experienced a different childhood than
I did. They were free!**

That, right there, is a great blessing - Freedom!

> *"The first time Uncle Mart left the Amish Church, he was just sixteen. During that time, he lived with my dad, Jonas. Within a few years, both of them returned to the Amish Church to get married. Many years later, however, when Uncle Mart was well-established in his cabinet making business, he left the Amish Church - this time for good. When I was ten years old, my father followed in Uncle Mart's footsteps, separating himself and his family from the Amish Church. Uncle Mart bought some land with my dad about an hour north. Our new farm had electricity, cars, everything! It was awesome!"*
>
> *~ Jonas Steury, nephew*

Tragedy Strikes!

In 1976, I was thirty-seven years old. Something happened that year that really shook my world. It's an afternoon I will never forget.

At the time, I owned a piece of property on a lake that I wanted to build a cabin on. One day, a friend of mine, who owned some property with an old dilapidated building on it, told me that if I took the structure down for him, I could keep any of the materials I could use. It was a big building with a lot of reusable 2x4s, so I took him up on his offer.

I asked my friend Alvin Graber, who worked for me, if he would help me with the job, and he agreed. When Memorial Day rolled around, me, Alvin, and my teenage son Melvin all took to the task at hand. First, we braced the building, then we began taking it apart, piece by piece.

Without warning, the building collapsed.
My son escaped, but Alvin was caught under the
rubble. In the end, my friend was left paralyzed.

Needless to say, this hindered our relationship. Alvin was left paralyzed for the rest of his life. There was insurance money, of course, but it wasn't nearly enough to compensate for such a tragedy. Regardless of his being confined to a wheelchair, I continued to employ Alvin, and he did whatever he was able to do. He came to work every day, and I kept him on the payroll.

A Terrible Shaking!

During the twelve months or so that followed, I carried around a very heavy burden. In my heart, I secretly blamed myself for what happened, and the guilt of it all was weighing me down. It was, after all, me who asked Alvin to help out, and I was the one calling the shots that day. I was certain we had braced everything properly, because I would never have moved ahead if that weren't so.

Eventually, I couldn't handle the weight of that burden another moment, let alone another day. The torment was too much for any man to bear.

One evening, while lying in bed beside my wife, despair wrapped itself around me and drained me of what little strength I had left. I was done!

That's when I got out of bed, got down on my knees, and wept before God. From the depths of my soul, I cried out to Him for help. Never in my life had I ever experienced such a place of desperation, but God met me right there in the midst my hopelessness and tears.

**I gave my life to God that night.
I gave him everything!**

*"I sought the LORD, and He heard me,
And delivered me from all my fears".
Psalm 34:4*

In return, God lifted that burden off my heart and replaced it with peace, an incredible peace. Somehow, He made it known to me that I didn't have to carry that load anymore - He would. That's exactly what Jesus died for - to carry our burdens. It's not like I didn't know that. I'd heard that message before at church, but now it was different. It was personal. God was personal.

When I finally got up off my knees, it was like I was a newborn person. The old me was gone and my life was new! Not only that, I never again looked at Alvin's tragedy the same. God had certainly shifted things, including my perspective. First and foremost, I saw that...

**It was through Alvin's tragedy that
God made Himself known to me.**

From that moment on, I realized I needed God! In His grace and mercy, Christ welcomed me into His family, and assured me that I would never have to do life alone, again.

**Alvin's tragedy also caused me
to thoroughly examine my life.**

After that night, I started talking to God in prayer. I read the Bible cover-to-cover, in search of answers to questions I'd never really asked before. It seemed like a whole new world opened up to me. It wasn't a religious thing, oh no. It was the start of a relationship with God in which He began leading and guiding me through life.

> *"I remember Dad's Bible continually laying open on the kitchen table from his morning spent with the LORD."*
>
> ~ *Marlene O'Donovan, daughter*

The Change

I don't know how long it took for others to notice that something was different about me. After all, it was an inner change, a heart transplant of sorts. All I know is that prior to this experience, I wasn't always the nicest person. Looking back, I was pretty aggressive at times and I never thought twice about it. From that point on, however, I began treating people better, more gently. Oh, there were still challenges in life that provoked me.

**I didn't always respond the right way, but
I knew the One I could go to for forgiveness.**

Over time, God smoothed out many of my rough edges.

A Sweet Goodbye

Many years later, Alvin took ill and was not expected to make it. During my visit with him, I asked him, *"Alvin, is there anything we need to make right between us?"*

"Oh Martin," he said, *"I forgave you a long time ago."*

I cried like a baby that day. Forgiveness is a wonderful thing!

Ephesians 4:32 says...

> *"Be kind to one another, tender-hearted,*
> *forgiving each other, just as God*
> *in Christ also has forgiven you."*

It wasn't long after that, only a day or so later, that I stood by Alvin's bedside when he took his last breath. He looked right at me, breathed his last, closed his eyes, and that was it. He didn't say anything, but I knew that was his way of saying goodbye. In an instant, the room was filled with the most magnificent peace. Truly, God was right there as Alvin passed from this world into eternity. My best friend was gone, but I know for certain that I will see him again one day in heaven.

A Yearning for More!

Soon after my born-again experience, our family changed churches again. Many things shifted during that time on my knees by my bed. I began seeing and experiencing things from a whole new perspective. The Bible came alive to me, and I yearned for a place to worship with others and grow in my faith even further.

Deep within, I sensed there was more!

I knew some people at *Sunrise Mennonite Church*, so one day, I decided to go and check out their service. To my delight, I discovered something wonderful there - a greater sense of freedom that I was inwardly longing for.

For one thing, the dress code was different. Where *King Church* had always adhered to a very plain dress code, here they dressed more normal - casual, but nice. Sunrise also had a full worship team that included instruments.

Music was always a part of who I was, but up until that point, I was never able to fully express myself in church worship. Oh, how I wanted to be able to personally engage in worship with instruments. You know it didn't take long for me to become a part of the *Sunrise* worship team. I loved that!

> *"Then King David spoke to the leaders of the Levites*
> *to appoint their brethren to be the singers accompanied*
> *by instruments of music, stringed instruments, harps,*
> *and cymbals, by raising the voice with resounding joy."*
> *1 Chronicles 15:16*

As small as those things may seem, they brought a real sense of completion to my faith. Finally, I was part of a family of believers who were in the same place in their spiritual life as I was. We were all on the same page, and with that unity came a greater sense of freedom and fulfillment.

CHAPTER 9

Tragedy

"Honor... your mother as the LORD your God has
commanded you, that your days may be long, and
that it may be well with you in the land which the
LORD your God is giving you."
Deuteronomy 5:16

The Accident

On May 21st, 1987, Marjorie was in a fatal car accident. To avoid an oncoming car, she turned off the road, went into a ditch, and hit a tree. Instantly, her neck was broken, and the angels whisked her home to be with the LORD.

Marjorie was the love of my life and the mother of my children. She was my hub - the center of our home. Everything revolved around her. We were married twenty-nine years and just like that, it was over - she was gone. By this time our older children had all left the roost, but the four youngest were still at home.

I was in Nashville, Tennessee at a woodworking auction with Furman Steury when it happened. The night prior, I called Marjorie to check on her and the kids. She told me she had an appointment the next morning with her chiropractor. The funny thing is, she kept saying, *"I have something I need to tell you, but I can't remember what it is!"* At the end of our call, I told her I loved her and we hung up.

The next day, while Furman and I were at the auction, an announcement came over the loud speaker requesting Martin Graber come to the office. I didn't have a clue what was going on or how they would even know me, but Furman and I headed to the office at once.

Our business partner, Meredith Yoder, was on the phone. Without beating around the bush, Meredith got straight to the point.

"Martin, your wife has had an accident and she's dead," he said.

It was such a shock, I literally dropped the phone. I asked if anyone was with Marjorie, wondering if my youngest son Lynn was with her in the car, but Meredith didn't know. When I came out of the office, I told Furman what happened. We needed to leave immediately.

I wasn't sure what to do, but I had a realtor friend, who lived in Nashville, named Charlie Harris. Right away, I called him and asked if he knew a way we could get home quickly. Charlie said he'd take care of it, and hired me a private plane.

One Regret

On the flight home, my life with Marjorie flashed through my mind like a movie. It was as if I relived every moment of our time together. I kept thinking of all the things I could have done better.

**All in all, I only had one regret.
I should have told Marjorie, *"I love you,"*
more often <u>and</u> in front of our children.**

My mom and dad never did that, and for some reason neither did I. Oh, how I wish the kids had heard me say that, then they'd know how much I loved their mom. That's so important, you know, because kids mimic their parents. I want my kids to know that's a good thing to do.

The Hospital

In two hours, I was back in Fort Wayne and heading to the hospital. When I arrived, I was met by family and friends. No time was wasted in taking me to the room where Marjorie was so I could be with her. Standing before her, I was in shock and a mess. There were lots of tears. I'd never experienced anything like that before, and it was hard to take it all in. The whole thing was surreal.

Part of me was angry. I was frustrated not knowing all the facts about what happened. I wanted to know the details, and insisted on seeing the police report. At some point, though, I came to the realization that knowing more wasn't going to bring Marjorie back. She was gone, and there was nothing that was going to change that.

> *"When Mart arrived at the hospital, I accompanied him when he went to see Marj. It was a rough night, and I was glad to be with my friend. For a long time, he cried, and I cried right along with him."*
>
> *~ Hank Byler, friend*

A Time of Great Grief

Afterwards, I went home where the younger kids were all waiting for me. Together, we cried and cried. For months, my youngest son slept next to me and cried himself to sleep, night after night.

It was a tough time for us all, a season of great grief, but we all knew that Mom - Marjorie - was a believer in Christ, and that she'd gone to be with Jesus in heaven.

We had a beautiful funeral service for Marjorie. There must have been three hundred people in attendance. She had a lot of friends, and they all turned out to give their condolences. Sadly, our Amish family did not attend.

As the days went on, Marjorie's loss weighed heavy on my heart, but even so, I was at peace. Mind you, that didn't mean I didn't have my share of meltdown moments. Still, God saw to it that I was comforted. I had to get back to work, and that helped me get my mind off things for a while. My daughter Rose came every day and helped with the children and the running of the house, until I got home at night.

"The night before she passed away, I was filling Dad and Mom's swimming pool with water, using a water tanker from the fire department. I was a volunteer fireman at the time. Mom wanted to make me something to eat before I left, but I was in a hurry. I said I couldn't, but she talked me into a having a grilled cheese sandwich. I'm so glad I stayed a little longer with her that day!"

~ Mel Graber, son

"Every year, during our Amish days, Dad would go elk or deer hunting and Mom would fill in for him doing the evening prayer with us kids. Before going upstairs to our bedrooms, we would all kneel by the living room couches and chairs and Mom would read the Prayer of Gratitude out of Dad's prayer book. That was our chance to say thank you to God for His blessings, provision, and protection. If any of us kids tried to be funny, Mom would just look at us with that gentle smile of hers. It's that same smile I got whenever I entered the room or went home for a visit. Oh, how I miss that smile!"

~ Marlin Graber, son.

The "To Do" List

Right after Marjorie's funeral, I made myself a *"To Do"* list of all the things I knew Marjorie had wanted me to do, that I simply hadn't gotten around to. There was some siding she wanted done on the barn, and a few handyman repairs that were needed in the basement. I felt better completing those things as I processed her parting and grieved the loss of it all.

I truly missed Marjorie. We were married for twenty-nine years, and she was my best friend - so loyal, a loving companion who was always by my side. She was also a good mother. With love, she taught our children well, cared for them with wisdom and grace, and ran the household with precision.

Of course, that doesn't even begin to describe who she was and all that she did, let alone mention the sweetness of her character and how that touched all our lives. I've said it time and time again, Marj was the hub of our family. She took care of everything and never complained. We had a peaceful home, a lovely family, and a lot of good friends. Marjorie was always welcoming and the perfect hostess to those who came to visit.

"Dad was the inviter, and Mom made it happen. He would say, 'I invited this person or that to come, and Mom would do whatever she needed to host and serve the crowd, large or small."

~ Marlin Graber, son

"Dad loved to entertain, so Mom was always in the kitchen fixing some sort of snack."

~ Rebecca Schwartz, daughter

"I remember Mom being a very shy, humble, and caring person. Just a few weeks before her passing, there was a singing at the church they attended. Mom wanted me to sing this song with her called, 'You Will Never Miss Your Mother Until She is Gone,' which, thank God, I actually did! Who knew?"

~ Mel Graber, son

The Bible says in *Proverbs 18:22,*

> *"He who finds a wife finds a good thing*
> *and obtains favor from the LORD."*

Marj was the epitome of that - the perfect example. She would be deeply missed by friends, her children, and especially by me.

"Mom was a good listener. She really cared about what you had to say. Whenever you needed anything, she was there. She was always there. After the car accident, that just stopped. From then on, it was different."

~ Rebecca Schwartz, daughter

CHAPTER 10

Married Again

A New Queen

As the days turned into weeks, the last thing on my mind was dating, let alone ever getting married again. After all, who on the earth would ever be interested in a man with ten kids? My focus in life became my family and navigating through our grief.

When July 4th rolled around, my friend Kenny invited me to go see the fireworks with him and his family, and I accepted. His sister Carol joined us and that was fine with me. We all went for dinner at *The Ponderosa* and then we headed to the ballfield for the celebration. It was a nice enough time, and I never thought much more of it.

Within weeks, my path crossed with Carol's once again, when I went to the ballpark where my son Lynn and my three grandsons were playing ball. She was there with two of her sons, Corey and Carlin. Looking back now, it's easy to see that God was still very much in total control of my life.

Snap! Just like that He ushered Carol front and center into my life with purpose.

Carol and I were by no means strangers. Aside from her being Kenny's sister, I was well-acquainted with her husband, Curt. He was a plumber that had done work for me on several occasions at the shop. Not only that, from time to time, he would stop by my property to shoot starlings from the locust trees with the guys. Sure enough, I had even installed the kitchen cabinets in their home.

A Tasteful Surprise!

One night when I was leaving the ball park to go home, I found a homemade cake laying on the front seat of my car. Beside it was a little note from Carol telling me she was praying for me in my time of grief. She also included a few handwritten Bible verses and some beautiful words of encouragement. Carol certainly understood how difficult it was for me, because she had lost her husband just a year earlier.

Not long after that, I found myself at the ball park again, and this time I needed a ride home. Carol offered to give me a ride and we quickly became friends. Another time, she invited me to her house with some friends for homemade pie. What's that old saying? *"The way to a man's heart is through his stomach."*

Without a doubt, Carol had a boldness about her. I used to tease her that I couldn't run fast enough to get away from her, but truth be told, if she hadn't reached out the way she did, I would never have said anything.

To date, I've only dated two women in
my life - Marjorie and Carol.
I dated them, and then I married them.

Carol said she knew I was *"The One"* after our very first date. I have to admit, I knew it, too! I took her out to a nice restaurant for dinner, but we talked so much, we never actually ate our meals.

Carol was a beautiful woman inside and out. Who knew I'd find my soul mate the second time around? A Christian, Carol was solid in her faith. Every time we got together, we made it a priority to pray with one another.

We'd only been seeing each other a couple months when Carol and I attended a conservative Christian conference together. That's when I asked her to marry me. Carol confessed to me that she had written a prayer to the LORD describing what she wanted in a husband, should the LORD choose to bring marriage her way a second time. Apparently, I was the manifestation of that prayer. Not only that, she used to always say to me, *"A man is not complete until he has a wife, then he gets his rib back."* I would agree with her on that.

Two Become One

On November 28, 1987, Carol and I were married at Sunrise Mennonite Church - six months after Marjorie's passing. This time, the wedding was more traditional. Carol wore a beautiful white wedding dress that she made herself, and I wore a tuxedo. Between us, we had seven girls and seven boys who gladly agreed to be our bridesmaids and groomsmen. Carol's oldest son, Curtis, was my best man. My daughter Wilma was Carol's matron of honor. Carol's daughter Cami was the maid of honor.

When Carol came down the aisle, she looked like an angel - so beautiful! Afterwards, we had a lovely reception and the next day, we went to Hawaii for two weeks for our honeymoon.

After being happily married to Marjorie all those years, I wasn't sure what to expect this time around. All I can say is that marrying Carol was delightfully different. We were older and more established. Merging our two households together, we didn't need a thing. On top of that, believe it or not, we had a smooth transition blending our families together. Carol was a wonderful mom and watched over all our kids like a mother hen.

All the Kids!

My kids, from oldest to youngest, were Wilma, Melvin, Marlin, Rebecca, (better known as "Becky"), Margaret, Rose, Martin Jr., ("Marty"), Marj, Marlene, and Lynn. Carol's kids were Curtis, Camilia who we called "Cami," Corey, and Carlin.

Together, Carol and I, and all our kids became a family.

---

*"Carol was a person of encouraging words,
never one to be negative!"*

~ Margaret Schwartz, daughter

*"Carol set a high precedence of positive guidance and
unwavering love. She could light up a room with her smile!
Her unconditional love and teachable moments made such
a positive impact on me and so many others. She had
the ability to uplift, strengthen, and remind you of the
undeniable power of God."*

~ Marjorie Vetter, daughter

*"I will always remember Mama Carol's smile.
I never saw her angry. She always assured us kids
that she wasn't taking our Mother's place."*

~ Wilma Zehr, daughter

*"Mom always had a soft word for any challenge
and a smile that would permeate through a room -
it was hard not to notice. She never spoke a cross word.
She'd always say, 'Your words matter, spend them carefully.'"*

~ Curt Graber, son

Every morning and in the evening before bed, Carol and I would lift up prayers together for our children and grandchildren. Surely, with eight kids in the home, it was God's grace and blessing that made it all come together so smoothly.

"An excellent wife is the crown of her husband."
Proverbs 12:4

People Take Precedence

One of the things I loved about Carol was the fact that she always had time for people. Her mantra was, *"Family First!"* and she stuck by it. Whenever the kids or the grandkids came to visit, Carol immediately stopped what she was doing and focused her full attention on them. She also took the time to write beautiful cards and letters to people. It was her ministry gift!

Carol was a happy person, positive, and always smiling. I never once heard her say a negative thing about anyone.

What can I say? She was a godly woman. To this day, I'm amazed when I look through her worn-out Bible. It's filled with notes, dates, things God spoke to her, and specific scriptures she gave to people.

> *"I remember Mom reading to me and Cami when we were young. She loved to tell Bible stories to us using easy words we could understand."*
> ~ *Curt Graber, son*

Christmas with Carol

Of all the holidays during the year, Christmas had to be Carol's favorite. For many years, she planned and prepared ahead of time for a very special day that included our younger kids and the grandchildren.

A few days before Christmas, all the pre-teens in our family would come to the house to help Carol put together the Christmas boxes for those in our town who were less fortunate. Each child was given the task, in advance, to bring something with them to put in the boxes. If they knew a family that needed something specific, they made it a point to always include it in the finely decorated package. When the boxes were completely filled, Carol and the kids delivered them throughout the neighborhood. What a joy this brought to Carol's heart! She also loved to get gifts for each person in the family, and would put a lot of thought into what she would get each one. On Christmas day, everyone got a Christmas gift!

"Carol loved children - especially her grandkids! At Christmas, she would throw a Birthday Party for Jesus and invite all the grandkids. Of course, there were always Christmas cookies to decorate, along with a craft or two. So much fun!"

~ Marjorie Vetter, daughter

"Whenever we played any kind of games with Mom, she never took it easy on us. We always had to try hard to beat her! She was also full of love. She never held back telling me she loved me, and with it always came a hug!

~ Corey Graber, son

World Travelers

" 'For I know the plans I have for you,' says the LORD, 'plans to prosper you and not to harm you, plans to give you a hope and a future.' "
Jeremiah 29:11 NIV

Carol and I loved traveling, and in time we would journey throughout the world to Tibet, China, Germany, Russia, Austria, Switzerland, South America, and more. Most of our trips were

Missions-minded. What joy it brought to our souls to be a part of what God was doing in other countries. Those endeavors were life-changing!

**One time I asked Carol which place she
liked the most. Lovingly, she told me that
her favorite place was wherever I was.**

During one of our trips, something very unusual happened. In Russia, there were a lot of poor children who lived in the streets and followed us wherever we went. The poverty there was heart-breaking. The kids were desperate to connect, and yearned for someone to take them away to a better place. Oh, how Carol and I wished we could have taken one of those kids home with us!

A few weeks after we arrived back in the States, we were contacted by someone asking if we would be interested in hosting a Russian student in our home. It didn't take us long to respond with a resounding, *"Yes!"*

Before long, Michael, a fourteen-year-old Russian boy, came and stayed with us for the next ten years. Michael did really well in high school and college. We simply treated him like one of our own kids. Truly, he was part of our family. After college, Michael moved to New York.

> *"Mart is a beautiful person! His love for the LORD,
> my Mother, us kids, not to mention the
> grands and greats is remarkable!"*
>
> ~ *Carlin Graber, son*

Florida Fun

Carol and I also loved to vacation in Florida. You just can't beat the warm sunny days and the cool breeze at the beach! Every year, we rented a condo at the *Surf and Racquet* on Siesta Key and brought the kids and grandkids with us. Eventually, we bought a house in Sarasota where our family could come year-round to visit and go to the beach. The kids all brought their friends along with them, and that was fine with us. The more the merrier!

Winter Snow

Indiana has some cold winters, but back then, we made the best of it. Our family loved to go skiing! Carol and I would pack the van full with our kids and their friends and off we'd go to the snow-covered mountains in Michigan. Oh, what fun we'd have. I think we did that several years in a row. One year, Carol sprained her ankle. After that, she preferred to just sit back and watch!

"I always enjoyed it when my family visited Florida - golfing with Grandpa, all the "Gator rides" he took us on, not to mention riding in his mustang convertible! Unforgettable!"

~ *A.J. Graber, grandson*

"As a boy, I loved visiting Grandpa's big house, swimming in his pool, and riding his ATUs all around the property - especially up and down the big dirt mound!"

~ *Dr. Darrin Schwartz, grandson*

"Some of my fondest childhood memories are of Grandpa and Carol taking all us kids - me Lynn, Carlin, Cory, and Rodney on ski trips to Bitter Sweet. Oh, what fun we had!"

~ *Loren Zehr, grandson*

CHAPTER 11

Dad

It All Started with One

Wilma, our first child, was born in the hospital. Thinking back now, I'm pretty sure Marj was in labor a whole day and a half. Oh, how I hated seeing her in so much pain. Whenever the doctor came in to check on her progress, I'd step out for a moment and return when his exam was complete.

In those days, the husband wasn't allowed in the delivery room during the actual birth, so while Marj was pushing, I was pacing the floor in the waiting room, hoping and praying that all would be okay.

When I was finally allowed back in the room, I was so proud of Marjorie, and so nervous about holding our little baby girl. Even though I had younger brothers and sisters, I'd never actually held any of them when they were newborns.

Responsibility

> **Finally, it was official! We were a family of three, and with that came the responsibility of providing for and taking care of my wife and child.**

It was definitely an exciting time, but for the most part, Marjorie was at home with the baby, while I worked all day. That's just the way it was, and before I knew it, I blinked my eyes and we were a family of twelve - Me, Marjorie and ten kids!

The Great Outdoors

Of course, living on a farm, there was plenty of fresh air and acres of land to run around on. I loved growing up on a farm, and it was great for all my kids as well. Together, we played softball and rode horses, and of course the kids all had their chores to do.

> *"With no more than a grade school education, my dad is well respected and a self-made success. He's always lived within his means, and we were always well taken care of. Through all the highs and lows of life, Dad has remained humble and kind. In his own words, "I am blessed!" He is appreciative of all that God has given him."*
>
> *~ Marjorie Vetter, daughter*

Parenting

Parenting ten kids had its challenges. Certainly, they didn't all do what they were told to do, all the time. Marjorie took care of the smaller incidents, and the larger issues were passed along to me. Really, we parented together. We were both on the same page and in agreement on how to discipline. I suppose many would say it was the *old school* way. That's all we knew. When the children were young, they sat on a chair in the corner for a time out. When they got older, they had privileges taken from them. On rare occasions, there was a spanking. All was done in love, never in anger.

Let be clear about something... as a father, I loved my kids and longed to have more time with them. I took them with me wherever I could, but when you work eight, ten, twelve hours a day, you're not always able to do that.

A Shop at Home

I always thought it would be wonderful to have the kids with me while I worked. Once I started building cabinets from home, that idea began to manifest. I rented out the farm, and put all my energy into building a business.

Teaching a Trade

Overall, my kids were good kids. I have no complaints. As they got older, pretty much every one of them came through the shop. As soon as they were able, they started out sweeping the floors and moved up to more advanced work. I never took their help for granted and paid them for the work they did.

> *"The worker deserves his wages."*
> *1 Timothy 5:18 NIV*

Of course, I wanted them to learn to make cabinets. They all had the desire to learn, so I taught them. It was important to me not only to have them around the shop, but to teach them a trade they could fall back on. I never thought about passing along the business to them one day. It was more about them learning a trade from which they could make a good living. All that said, the business was all the better for it! There's no doubt in my mind that without them, *Dutch Made* wouldn't have grown as fast as it did.

Embracing Integrity

My kids all knew what to do, and I could always count on them to finish the job. When we had a deadline, we all pulled together to get it done, staying late if need be, to get it delivered on time.

> **I taught my kids that if you promise something,**
> **you deliver. That kind of dedication establishes**
> **integrity and a good work ethic.**

To be honest, cabinet building is a fun thing. Even today, I enjoy it. It broadens your horizon of what you can do, because you become a *Finish Carpenter*. You know how to paint. You know all the facets that are part of the process. I'm sure some of them today may be better at it than I ever was.

> *"Working for Martin for almost thirty years, I
> got to know him pretty well. His drive to succeed
> in business is outstanding! First of all, age is only a
> number to Martin. If there's a will, there's always a way!
> Second, it doesn't matter if something is not popular.
> No matter what, Martin will find a way to 'get 'er done!'"*
>
> ~ *Doris Graber, daughter-in-law*
>
> *"Something that stands out to me about Grandpa
> is his will to get anything done he puts his mind to.
> He's amazing!"*
>
> ~ *Hannah Eicher, granddaughter*

The Second Time Around

When Carol and I got married, for a while there, we had eight kids in the house, half of which were teenagers, which in itself had its challenges. For the most part, things flowed fairly smoothly, but you have to remember my kids had just lost their mother, and Carol's kids had just lost their father the year prior.

**I suppose you could say we were
a family of wounded hearts,
and every child grieved differently.**

Some flowed better than others and some acted out. Needless to say, Carol and I read a lot of books about blended families, gleaning from the pages all the wisdom we could get. We stayed positive, and we agreed that we would support one another in parenting. Whether she disciplined the kids or I did, we always stood behind what the other did.

Learning to Flow!

Being a father is a very important role and it carries with it an enormous responsibility. By no means do I claim to have been an expert. I was learning to flow myself one day to the next. I asked the LORD for help all the time - for wisdom and direction on how to be the man He desired me to be in my marriage, in my family, and in my business. I wouldn't have made it without Him.

"If any of you lacks wisdom, let him ask of God,
who gives to all liberally and without reproach,
and it will be given to him."
James 1:5

> *"In 1987, after the passing of my father, Mart strode into my life as a knight in shining armor for my mother, Carol, in her greatest time of need. His willing gifts of wisdom and knowledge have empowered and perpetuated through my adult life. Over the years, Mart has transcended from normal stepfather to a true father figure. I so appreciate his noble humbleness, leadership, and integrity in both family and business, not to mention his willingness to help all those around him!"*
>
> *~ Curtis Graber, son*
>
> *"Mart and I spent an entire year building my house and shop. I still can't believe we took on a job of that scale, but in the end, we successfully accomplished our goal!"*
>
> *~ Carlin Graber, son*

A Father Figure

Of course, I wanted Carol's kids to like me, but more importantly, I had a God-given responsibility to be the man of the house, and a father figure to all the children - hers and mine. That said, there were times when I had to be firm. That wasn't always easy, but I did my best to do it in a most-loving way. Carol and I prayed a lot too. In time, all her kids ended up calling me Dad. They weren't required to do that, but I have to say, it meant so much to me when they did. It really made me feel good.

"Around the time Mart and my mom got married, Mart told me, 'I don't want to replace your dad.' When I was younger, I didn't always see eye-to-eye with Mart and was often angry with him, but now, I appreciate and love him very much. He has always treated me well and made sure I knew he cared for me. For many years now, I call him my dad."

- Corey Graber, son

Means the world to me!
Accepts me as I am.
Rejoices in the LORD!
Takes time for his family.
Insightful, speaks the truth!
Never gives up! Stays active.

I'm so thankful Martin has been a father to me. I love you Mart!

~ Julia Renee Graber, daughter-in-law

One Big Family

It wouldn't be fair to give the impression that Carol and I did it all on our own. By this time, my older kids were all married and starting families of their own. Even so, they were quick to offer support and help. Whenever Carol and I had someplace to go, our kids stayed with Wilma. She loved taking care of them.

Really, what it comes down to is this:
Over time, the Hand of God wove
our families together into ONE.

Today, our extended family is quite large. The kids all have kids of their own, and their kids have kids. Not a day goes by that I don't think about them and what they are doing. It gives me lots to talk to the LORD about.

Marriage and family are by no means easy,
but the blessings they produce are the
ones we treasure most in life!

Released to God's Care

My family is always in my prayers. I think they all know that. Most importantly, I have released them to God, knowing that He will have His way in all their lives - the kids, the grandkids, and the great-grandkids. If there's one thing I know, it's that I can't live their lives for them. I can't control them, nor do I want to. Each one is free to live their own life. That said, I trust God to work in their lives, just like He did in mine, making Himself known along the way, and bringing them to where He wants them to be. He has a plan for each one of them, and to them my advice is this:

Don't try to do life alone.
Instead, walk and talk with God.
It's such a better way!

At this point, my job is to make sure they know I love them, tell them about Jesus, and encourage them to never to give up!

> *"I've had the privilege of looking up to a man who never ceases to give God glory in everything he does. He's a generous man, yet humble, never blinking at the opportunity to lend someone a helping hand!"*
>
> *~ Hannah Eicher, granddaughter*

> *"My grandpa, alongside my parents, is the most influential person in my life. He has taught me so much, and our relationship is one I cherish most. He's always there for me, and he always has this way of making me feel special. Words will never be enough to say how much he means to me. I love you, Grandpa!"*
>
> *~ Karla Graber, granddaughter*

> *"Grandpa is the man I dream of growing up to be! When I'm around him, I feel loved and appreciated, because he genuinely cares for his family. Most of all, Grandpa has always lived his life for Jesus. He's been a role model for me to walk that same path of faith. To me and many others, Grandpa is an excellent example of God's unconditional love."*
>
> *~Jaeden Lengacher, grandson*

> *"You just have to look into Grandpa's eyes to know he loves you so very much!"*
>
> *~ Celina Jones, granddaughter*

CHAPTER 12

Cut Short

During the thirty-three years I was married to Carol, two of our children died prematurely. Carol's daughter Cami died of a brain tumor, and my son, Marty, battled with depression and ultimately took his own life.

Cami

Cami was sixteen when Carol and I got married. She was Carol's second child, the oldest girl. I'll never forget how excited Cami was about us getting married. More than anything, she wanted her mother to be happy. Being a bit protective of her mom, Cami put together a list of rules for me to abide by when we were dating. One was "No kissing! Just holding hands." Another was making sure that I got Carol home from a date by midnight.

Cami and I always got along well. At one point, she came and worked for me as my secretary for seven years. She was always so full of fun and did her job well.

Cami grew up to be a beautiful young woman and on her wedding day, I proudly walked her down the aisle as if she were my own daughter. In my mind, she was. She was such a beautiful bride. In time, she and Fabian had two wonderful children.

One Wednesday in 2005, tragedy struck quite unexpectedly. Cami experienced a horrendous headache and suddenly became seriously ill. That morning, while caring for her children ages one and three, Cami keeled over and lost consciousness. In the hospital, it was discovered that she had a tumor on her brain stem. She never did regain consciousness. On Friday, May 21st, Cami passed away. I couldn't believe it! May 21st was the very same date that my first wife Marj passed away.

With no warning and no time to do anything, we were all shocked. Carol went and stayed with Fabian and the kids for a couple weeks, helping out any way she could. In addition to all that, Fabian's mother passed away that December. Carol and I were more than happy to take the kids with us to Florida that winter, and Fabian came down to visit them often. Cami's death was hard. The children cried for their mommy for a long time.

> *"Over the years, Grandpa Graber's beneficial nuggets of wisdom and discernment have guided so many of us through life. He's been a godsend during some very rough times, and I praise the LORD for him and for the blessing he has been to me personally."*
>
> *~ Fabian Lengacher, son-in-law*
>
> *"Ever since my mom passed away, Grandma and Grandpa Graber have always made sure my brother and I were well taken care of. Often, they'd tell me wonderful stories about Mom, so that I would never forget her. I love them for that! Grandpa Graber is one of my biggest supporters - so caring and such an encouragement to me."*
>
> *~Averi Lengacher, granddaughter*

Marty

Growing up, my son Marty was the total image of me when I was young - aggressive and not the best listener, but a hard worker all the same. After school, he worked with me at the cabinetry shop putting doors together, and did a fine job!

Young and ambitious, Marty was just a teenager when he told me he wanted to buy himself a motorcycle. Concerned about his safety, I said no, and encouraged him to save his money for a car instead. By the time he was sixteen, he'd saved up enough money to buy himself a brand-new *Trans Am*.

That sounds impressive, but it really wasn't such a good idea. A *Trans Am* isn't the right car for a young man. It made a lot of people jealous. Before long, Marty was in with the wrong crowd, drinking beer, and doing cocaine. Too much money at a young age can lead to trouble.

At sixteen, Marty joined the fire department. He'd always looked up to his older brother who worked there and decided to follow in his footsteps. One day, when Marty was in his early twenties, he answered a call to respond to a tragic car accident, only to discover that it was his mother in the car. He was the first to respond on the scene, and when he arrived Marjorie had already passed.

Two weeks earlier, Marj had asked Marty if she could use his *Trans Am* to go to the grocery store and do some errands, and he said yes. Marty kept his car meticulous and was not happy when she returned it and it was not up to his standards. He had a few tense moments and words with her and never got the chance to apologize to her for his harshness. In my heart, I think that laid the founda-tion for Marty's battle with depression.

Sometimes, Marty was okay, and sometimes he wasn't so good. His alcohol and cocaine use only magnified his painful struggle. Eventually, he overdosed and ended up in rehab.

On several occasions, Marty's girlfriend, Jennifer, stopped by the house to see Carol and I, requesting prayer. She knew Marty had a problem - the drugs had a grip on him, he couldn't seem to shake.

One time, Carol and I thought Marty was going to die, so we called 911 and he was taken back to rehab to detox. That's when the doctor put him on anti-depressants.

A few years later, Marty and Jennifer got married. Unfortunately, their marriage suffered because of Marty's alcohol and drug abuse. Regardless, they had four beautiful children. Even so, Marty's depression continued as did his struggle with alcohol and drugs.

Several years later, a doctor, once again, prescribed Marty antidepressants. For a while there, Marty seemed to respond well to them. Unfortunately, it was short-lived. When he started feeling better, he stopped taking his meds, and six weeks later he was gone.

Life is a precious gift from God, but
when darkness and depression move
in, sometimes people forget that.

On May 28, 2008 - two years after Cami died - Marty gave in to his battle with depression and took his own life.

"Grandpa's life and love for God has spoken volumes to me over the years, especially when it comes to his prayers, persistence, and the extension of God's grace to me personally - many times over.

Grandpa's son Marty was my uncle, but he wasn't that much older than me. We were friends... best friends! Over the years, we did a lot of things together - good and bad. When Marty died, I was totally devastated and my life quickly spiraled out of control.

<u>BUT GRANDPA NEVER GAVE UP ON ME!</u>

By the grace of God, Grandpa saw past the error of my ways and saw someone better, someone that even I couldn't see at the time. His ability to extend grace not only changed my life, it changed me. It changed me from the inside-out!

~ Loren Zehr, grandson

At the viewing, we noticed that Marty's hands were severely bruised, and asked the funeral director about it. He believed that Marty most likely had regrets about his attempt to hang himself. It appeared he struggled to free himself at the last minute, but was unsuccessful. That little detail brought us some peace of mind.

It was a very sad time. Of course, family and friends came out to offer their condolences and support. My brother-in-law Jonas, Marjorie's brother, came to the viewing and was killed in a car accident the very next day. We were devastated!

> *"Thank you for introducing me to salvation. Over the years, I've attributed so much of my faith and walk with Jesus to your personal example and wisdom. In turn, my children have been raised in the knowledge of Christ. What a lovely day that will be stepping into Heaven! I have you and Carol to thank for it! Know that you are forever in my heart."*
>
> *~ Jenny Graber, daughter-in-law*

A Tearful Dream

A year or so later, Carol and I were in Florida, and our friends, Hank and Joann Byler were staying with us for a couple weeks. One Sunday morning while resting, I had fallen asleep and to Carol's surprise, she noticed I was crying. Caught up in a dream, I saw my son Marty standing in heaven amidst a group of people who were singing a familiar old church song:

> *"Turn Your Eyes Upon Jesus.*
> *Look full in His wonderful face.*
> *And the things of earth will grow strangely dim,*
> *In the light of His glory and grace."*

I was so moved by what I saw, I began to cry bittersweet tears.

Soon after, a woman from our church called me, completely out of the blue, insisting she needed to tell me something. *"The LORD showed me that Marty is in Heaven!"* she declared. To our astonishment, that was the whole purpose of her phone call.

For many years, Marty attended *Sunrise Mennonite Church* where he accepted Jesus as his LORD and Savior and was water baptized. In my heart, I believe Marty went to be with the LORD, and one day, I will see him again. The dream, the random phone call, the evidence of his bruised hands attempting to reverse his decision to take his own life, along with the knowledge of his accepting Christ into his life and his openness for prayer, are all affirmations of that.

CHAPTER 13

Fullness

Baptism by Immersion

For years, my friend Hank Byler and I talked about doing something. We wanted to be water baptized by immersion. That's when your whole body is dunked under the water.

In the Amish Church, when people become official church members, they are water baptized by sprinkling. If you remember, joining the church and being water baptized was a pre-requisite to my marrying Marjorie. That said, on my wedding day, I was sprinkled with water by the Amish minister.

One day, I was visiting my friend Wayne Weaver's church, *Oasis.* My pastor, Lael Barkman, was preaching at the meeting there. That's when I told Lael that I wanted to be water baptized by immersion.

The first thing he said was, *"What do you suppose people will think if you do that?"*

I told him, *"I don't care what people think. It's what I feel in my heart that I need to do!"*

Lael said he'd get back to me, but the weeks went by and I never heard from him on the matter. Then, one Sunday, I stood up during church and explained to the congregation what was happening in my heart, and how I wanted to be rebaptized by immersion. I'm pretty timid, you know. The whole thing was like a dream, and totally unplanned. I didn't know what I was doing. Something, or Someone led me up to the front of the church to do that. I'm pretty sure it was the Holy Spirit.

**The Mennonite congregation was stunned!
I said what the LORD had put on my heart
to say, I sat back down in my seat, and for
a moment everything was quiet.**

To my surprise, six more people stood up, went to the front, and reiterated the exact same thing. They wanted to be baptized by immersion, too! I had no idea that anybody else in our church was feeling the same way I was. In the end, everyone in our church, the entire congregation, ended up getting baptized by immersion, even Carol. Not all at one time, of course, but little by little.

**Who would have known that by standing up and
humbly sharing my heart, God would release
that desire in the hearts of everyone?**

The day of my baptism got closer and closer, and boy was I excited! The plan was to have it done in our backyard swimming pool after Sunday morning church. We invited our family and a few friends to be there to celebrate with us. No one ever suspected tragedy to surround that day.

Earlier that week, you see, was when Marty died. His funeral was set for that Friday, and my pastor called suggesting I put off the baptism to another time. As thoughtful as that was, I didn't want to wait.

Then my brother-in-law Jonas died in the car accident! His funeral was scheduled for the following Monday. Again, the pastor called and asked if I wanted to put the baptism off. Of course, with everything that had happened, it would certainly be understandable.

"No!" I said. *"We can't do that! That's exactly what the devil would want. He doesn't like the idea of me getting baptized by immersion."*

So, we buried my son on the Friday, and my brother-in-law on the Monday. Right in between the two, I was water baptized.

**Right in the middle of these two tragic losses,
God did something wonderful! It was only in His
strength and by His grace that it all came together.**

With my family and friends gathered 'round the swimming pool, under the water I went! When I came up, it was as if the heavens opened up. The whole sky seemed to light up! In that moment, the Holy Spirit came upon me, and a glorious feeling came over me. Never before had I felt so clean and so whole. It was a completeness in God and a knowing that there was nothing further I needed to do.

*"Just as Jesus was coming up out of the water,
He saw heaven being torn open, and the Spirit
descending on Him like a dove, and a voice
came from heaven: 'You are My Son, whom I
love; with You I am well-pleased.'"
Mark 1:10-11 NIV*

"Mart and I talked about baptism by immersion for close to three years! Then, one day, to my surprise, he just stood up in church and shared his heart with everyone! When the day arrived for Martin to be water baptized, you bet I was in the pool being baptized, too!"

~ Hank Byler, friend

Set Free from Abuse

Freedom comes in many different ways. Sometimes we yearn for it, even fight for it, and when it finally happens, we're grateful. Other times, we don't even realize that we're in bondage until someone points it out to us. There's an old saying...

**"God works in mysterious ways,
His wonders to perform."**

When I was twelve years old, I was abused by a boy who was sixteen. One day, we were working the farm together and our dads sent us out into the fields to prepare the ground for seed. That's when the boy first took advantage of me. He had me do things that weren't right. This lasted two to three years. Every time my father mentioned I'd be working with the boy, my insides cringed.

**I hated the thought of something happening,
and it always did. I was so intimidated by him.**

One time, I mustered up the courage to say something to the boy, but he just laughed. I didn't know anything and he seemed to know everything. Eventually, I got older and refused to do those things. The boy got older, too, and began hanging out with an older crowd.

The Bible says in *Isaiah 61:1...*

*"The Spirit of the LORD is upon Me...
To proclaim liberty to the captives,
And the opening of the prison
to those who are bound."*

God Reveals to Heal

For many decades, I never said a thing to anyone. I pushed it to the back of my mind hoping I'd just forget about it. Then one day, a traveling minister, Reuben Beachy, came to our church to hold meetings. Afterwards, we invited Reuben to our home to join us for a meal and some fellowship.

At the end of our time together, Reuben asked if he could pray a blessing over Carol and I before he left, and we agreed to it. In the middle of the prayer, however, Reuben stopped short, looked at me, and said he felt there was someone or something that had a hold on me.

At first, I wasn't sure what Reuben was referring to, but then he went on to give a description of what God was revealing to him. To my astonishment, his account was undeniable. I knew immediately who Reuben was talking about, for as he spoke, those dreadful memories from my childhood all came flooding back.

Prior to all this, I had never said anything to Reuben or anyone else about the abuse. Reuben went on to assure me that God had revealed it in order to set me free and bring healing. Reuben went on to pray a prayer of release over me, and truly I was set free from the hold that man from my past had on me.

"He who the Son sets free is free indeed."
John 8:36

A few years ago, I attended a local, charitable banquet. Arriving late, I took the only seat that was available. Lo and behold, the man sitting beside me was that perpetrator from my youth. I was surprised that he didn't even know who I was. It made me wonder if he had dementia. How else could a man not remember the one he violated in childhood? So many questions flooded my mind. Had he suppressed those memories? Maybe I wasn't the only one he hurt? Was he, himself, a victim? Needless to say, I didn't sit there long. I left the banquet early. Since then, the man has died.

"For I have satisfied the weary soul, and
I have replenished every sorrowful soul."
Jeremiah 31:25

I share this story with purpose. Perhaps there is someone from your past who hurt you badly. Sometimes we don't realize that those kind of childhood atrocities can grab hold of one's heart in such a way that we become fearful, or hesitant, or guarded. God doesn't want us to live bound up in that. He has come to set us free, and that freedom is but a prayer away.

"For He has not despised or abhorred the affliction
of the afflicted; Nor has He hidden His face from Him:
But when He cried to Him, He heard.
Psalm 22:24

The Buyout of the Business

As I mentioned earlier, *Dutch Made Cabinetry* had three business partners. After many years, the day came when Furman and Meredith wanted to sell, but I didn't. They already had a buyer and had taken a down payment. I was left thinking, *"This is the end of the road."*

That spring, Carol's first husband's father, Ervin, came to visit the grandkids. Over the years, he and I had become friends. Even now, I can still recall the details of that day. Carol and I were sitting at the table deciding what we were going to do when the business was sold. When Ervin arrived, he sensed we were troubled over something and straight out asked, *"What's wrong?"* After filling him in on the situation at hand, Ervin remarked confidently, *"Well then, you just need to buy them out!"*

Of course, I didn't have a million dollars to buy them out, but Ervin insisted that I go to the bank, talk to my accountant, and let them work it out. So, that's exactly what I did. To my surprise, they put together a ten-year buyout plan and it was accepted!

"And whatever you do, in word or deed, do all
in the name of the LORD Jesus, giving thanks to
God the Father through Him."
Colossians 3:13

Ervin's visit turned out to be such a divine connection. Without his encouragement and advice, I would never have come up with that idea on my own, let alone moved forward with it.

I'm convinced that God sets us up at key crossroads in our lives. Not only that, but after I bought the business, it prospered significantly. For sure, I don't understand it all, but God does.

When God is your Life Partner,
He's intricately involved in the details of
everything - your marriage, your family,
your health and wellbeing, your business,
your finances, your life!

"To me, my Uncle Mart is a great leader, and I
believe his faith has a lot to do with his success!"

~ Jonas Steury, nephew

Church Eldership

"And they cast their lots, and the lot fell on Matthias,
and he was numbered with the eleven apostles."
Acts. 1:26

In the Mennonite church that Carol and I attended, every so often, the congregation would vote in elders or overseers. People would submit their nominees and ultimately, it would come down to three people with the most votes. One year, I was one of the three.

On the platform, at the front of the church, were three books. Hidden inside one of them was a piece of paper that clearly stated, *"You're chosen!"* One by one, the three finalists went up to the front and chose a book.

I was the third person in line, so the two before me chose their books and I took the one remaining. It didn't really matter, because the Holy Spirit had already whispered in my ear, *"It's going to be you, Martin!"*

To be honest, I'm not sure I wanted the job. The idea of being an elder scared me, because I knew it had its challenges. Each elder was responsible for sharing scriptures and stories during the weekly church services. If corrections needed to be made among the congregation, the elders had to deal with those matters. I don't particularly like conflict and confrontation, so I knew that would be hard for me. In addition to all that, there were monthly leadership meetings with the pastor to discuss church business.
I wasn't sure the job was for me, but God seemed to have a different opinion.

Sometimes, God sets you up for the very thing
that you would personally choose not to do.

Sure enough, I stepped onto the platform with the other two candidates, we opened our books, and there before me were the words, *"You're chosen!"*

I must say, the ten years that followed were a challenging yet blessed time in my life. It was not an easy job, and certainly I was stretched. For one thing, I had to stay in God's Word and pray daily in order to hear from God and properly carry out my duties. More than a few times, I wept over matters in prayer and petition. There were times I wanted to leave, but Carol was always there to encourage me and remind me that I was divinely chosen for a purpose. As hard as it was, the LORD used it to mold and shape me into the man of God He wanted me to be.

"Dad's advice is desired by most everyone that knows him."

~ Marlin Graber, son

"Martin personifies 1 Thessalonians 5:11 - 'Encourage one another and build one another up.' Martin values people! He's what I call a Discerner of Gifts. He observes people's strengths, then activates them by giving them an opportunity to let their gifts shine. He has a knack for sitting and talking with people, all while helping them work through things.

~ Joann Byler, friend

"To describe Mart as humble would be a complete understatement. To live a life of pursuit, stewardship, and godliness, displayed as he has, would take an entire lifetime of growth. Yet in all the years, from the roots, to the rings, to the branches, you can see the story of the tornadoes he has withstood and still see the sign of fruit to bear the next season. Grandpa was a seed planted in fertile soil!"
(Matthew 13:8)

~ Quentin Graber, grandson

"Fear not, for I am with you;
Be not dismayed, for I am your God.
I will strengthen you, Yes, I will help you,
I will uphold you with My righteous right hand."
Isaiah 41:10

CHAPTER 14

Goodbye

A Miracle

In 2012, it was discovered that Carol had a brain tumor. For two years, she lived day-by-day, knowing her departure was at hand. Radiation treatments ushered in significant weight loss, and Carol put her affairs in order, even planning her own funeral.

Two years passed, and the doctors suspected that Carol had another tumor and wanted to do a biopsy. We were advised to get a second opinion, so we made an appointment with Florida University Medical Center.

Anointing and Prayer

Before Carol went for the new tests and scans, she asked our dear friend, Reuben Beachy, to come to our home, anoint her with oil, and pray over her. It was her way of making room for God to do something. Reuben wasted no time in bringing a prayer team by the house to pray for healing, health, and wellness.

> *"Is anyone among you sick? Let him call for the*
> *elders of the church and let them pray over him,*
> *anointing him with oil in the name of the LORD."*
> *James 5:14*

A few days later, Carol and I went and met with twelve specialists at Florida University. The doctors thoroughly examined Carol and carried out all the various tests and scans that were needed. After collaborating with one another, they called us at home with their final conclusion. I can't tell you how overjoyed we were when they told us there was absolutely no reoccurrence of the tumor. What they thought was a tumor turned out to be scar tissue from the radiation.

If you want to know what I think, I think the *scar tissue* was the place where God divinely touched her with His healing power. I say that because some of the symptoms Carol was experiencing immediately went away after that time of prayer with Reuben. The biggest issue Carol had was her constant sickness and weight loss. After every meal, she was sick to her stomach, to the point of losing thirty pounds. That was a consistent symptom for the longest time, but the day after the anointing, all that changed for the better. For the first time in a long time, Carol was able to keep food down without throwing up.

Make no mistake, we thought for sure that Carol was on her way out. God did something very special that night and we are set on giving God all the glory for it.

**The fact that Carol gained six more years
was nothing short of a miracle!**

We never stopped praising God for that blessing of extended time.

2 Kings 20:5-6 says it best...

> *"I have heard your prayer. I have seen your tears;
> Surely, I will heal you... I will add to your days..."*

Time to Sell

In 2019, I made the decision to sell *Dutch Made,* so I could spend more time with my wife, caring for her in the best possible way. Each day was precious to me! In the end, I got a full year and a half with her. Oh, how glad I was for that! Then one day in December of 2020, Carol suffered a massive heart attack and went home to be with the LORD. We'd been married thirty-three years.

Our Last Years Together

In all our years together, Indiana was our home. During the last two years of Carol's life, a senior care helper named Katie came to the house three times a week for half days to help Carol out. Carol loved her companionship! Together, they'd go out shopping, go to the nail and hair salon, and exercise at the gym. When they came home later in the day, I'd take over, caring for Carol the rest of the time.

Back to the Hospital

After the brain surgery in 2012, Carol struggled with her sugar, but it got corrected to where she didn't need to take medication for it anymore. Unfortunately, for a couple months in those last days, that struggle returned. It was the evening of Friday, December 19th, when I discovered that Carol's sugar level was super high. I didn't know what to do, so my daughter Rose and I brought her to the hospital.

By the time we arrived, Carol had gotten worse. The doctors did tests and told me she had a massive heart attack. They admitted her overnight, and I stayed by her bedside.

The next day, the doctors informed us that Carol wasn't going to make it. In their examination, they discovered that Carol had experienced seven heart attacks over the years that we never knew about. Three or four of them were just in the last two years. Her heart was now functioning at a mere ten percent. They also tested her for COVID. The results were positive, even though she had no COVID symptoms and I never came down with it myself.

Right away, I wanted to take Carol home, because that would allow me to stay with her around the clock, and the family could all be with her. In discussing it with the family, however, it was decided that Carol would get better medical care if she stayed in the hospital. At that time, two of her kids were out of state, trying to get back to see their mom before she passed, and the hospital was doing everything they could to keep Carol alive so they could see her. All in all, it was a difficult decision to make, but we moved her to the hospital's hospice unit. They kept Carol alive for a day and a half, and the kids did get to the hospital in time to say their goodbyes.

Unfortunately, because of the hospital's COVID policy, I was only allowed to stay with Carol from 8 a.m. to 10 p.m. In addition to that, only two people were allowed in her room at any given time, so of course, we all took turns.

Our time in the hospital was hard. Carol was awake for most of it, but we all knew that her time was short. We all said our goodbyes and cried a lot of tears.

During one of our conversations, Carol and I discussed the burial. Prior to all this, we acquired a family plot in the church cemetery. Carol's first husband, Curtis, is on one end, then Carol, an open place for me, then Marjorie. That's exactly the way we wanted it.

That night at precisely 10:00 I was instructed by the hospital staff that I had to leave. Reluctantly, and with tears in my eyes, I said goodnight and waved to Carol as I went out the door.

I no sooner arrived home and the phone rang. It had been just over an hour and the hospital was calling for me to return. By the time I arrived back there, Carol was gone.

There's nothing I could have done to change the situation, but I wished I could have been there, holding her hand, when the angels came for her.

On the evening of Monday, December 21, 2020, Carol passed away from a massive heart attack. Surprisingly, her death certificate said, "Complications from COVID Pneumonia."

In my heart, I know that the sugar issues she was fighting managed to get a grip on her that she couldn't escape. That, along with all the hidden heart attacks she'd experienced did her in. All in all, we were blessed by God with eight extra years! Those years after the brain surgery had their challenges, but it was still a precious gift from God.

"I can't think of Carol and not think of this Bible verse...

"And He said to me, 'My grace is sufficient for you, for My strength is made perfect in weakness.' Therefore, most gladly I will rather boast in my infirmities, that the power of Christ may rest upon me. Therefore, I take pleasure in infirmities, in reproaches in needs, in persecutions, in distresses, for Christ's sake. For when I am weak, then I am strong."
2 Corinthians 12:9-10

~ Marjorie Vetter, daughter

The Funeral

It was a beautiful funeral - truly a celebration of Carol's life. Even so, it was very hard for me to let her go. We always said we'd go together, but she didn't listen.

Because of the COVID pandemic at hand, many places didn't allow funerals during that time. In Indiana, we were able to have a funeral, but for the most part, we were on our own to run things. The senior pastor at my church, Lael Barkman, helped me put things together, and Pastor Dan Bontrager did the service. Over three hundred people attended.

One evening, shortly after Carol's funeral, I caught myself talking to Carol. Sometimes, that's how we process our grief.

"Can she hear me, LORD?" I whispered.

Suddenly, there was a strange sound in the bedroom. For a moment, it made me think that someone was moving something around in there. Was it a sign of sorts? I can't say for sure, but I talked a lot with her during that time.

When you love someone deeply, it's really hard to let go, but step by step, one day at a time, we eventually fully release them to God, knowing that we will someday be reunited with them.

All in all, I had thirty-three wonderful years with Carol, and every one of them was a treasure.

A Sweet Reminder

My dear friend, Richard Miller, died December 12 and Carol died December 21st. One day while going through some paperwork, I found a sympathy card that Carol wrote to Richard's wife, Clara. Carol was always doing things like that. It was like a ministry. What a bittersweet reminder of my kind-hearted wife. Not long after, I brought the card by Clara's house when I offered my condolences.

"With all the trials our family went through, I certainly saw Dad at some of the lowest times of his life. Even still, he would lift his head and say, 'The joy of the LORD is my strength!' What a living testimony that is!

To see how he loved my Mom and then how he cared for Carol through her health journey - Dad wasn't perfect, none of us are, but we still loved each other through it all!"

~ Wilma Zehr, daughter

Special Friends

Losing a spouse creates a vacancy, not just in one's heart, but in one's life. All those years, my closest friend was continually by my side, then suddenly there was a deep void. No matter how busy I kept myself, emptiness haunted me. It's easy to be lonely, even though you're surrounded by family and friends.

Life isn't meant to be empty.
It's meant to be full.

Some time has passed since that day I dropped off the card at Clara's. Since then, she and I have spent a lot of time together talking, going places, and visiting family and friends. We enjoy one another's company and have become close, special friends, and companions. My heart and life are beginning to fill up again, and with that, there's a renewed happiness.

"And the LORD God said,
'It is not good that man should be alone...'"
Genesis 2:18

"Behold, the former things have come
to pass, and new things I declare:
Before they spring forth, I tell you of them.
Behold, I will do a new thing! Now it shall
spring forth; Shall you not know it?"
Isaiah 42:9; 43:19

"The steps of a good man
are ordered by the LORD,
And He delights in his way.
Though he fall, he shall not be
utterly cast down; for the LORD
upholds him with His hand."
Psalm 37:23-24

"A man's heart plans his way,
But the LORD directs his steps."
Proverbs 16:9

CHAPTER 15

Extended

"With long life I will satisfy him,
and show him My salvation."
Psalm 91:16

Back and Forth

Today, I spend my time going back and forth from Indiana to Florida. The warm weather of sunny Sarasota is more appealing to me these days, but I still enjoy spending time with my family up north. They like to visit Florida as well, so it's the best of two worlds. In the midst of the grieving, I can't help but wonder what God has in store for me next. Meanwhile, I'm writing this book, and there's still a few important things I need to say.

God Protects

To date, I've been in three car accidents that should have been fatal. Each time, God protected me and I came out of them with mere scratches. Looking back now, there's no way I should have survived these accidents, but for the grace of God.

The first of these accidents happened when I was married to Marj. One day, my son Marty and I took a ride to one of my farms in Angola. On the way home, I came around a curve when suddenly, a car coming from the other direction crossed over the center line and was headed straight for us. Without hesitating, I turned the wheel to the right to avoid a head on collision, and went off the berm. The car flipped and landed in a ditch. Amazingly, Marty and I walked away unscathed. Meanwhile, the other driver just continued on his way, never stopping. I didn't think much of it at the time. I was just glad we were both okay.

"But you, O LORD, are a shield for me..."
Psalm 3:3

Years later, I was heading home from Nashville after visiting with my other son, Lynn. It was cold that night, and my grandson Kyle was with me. He was in his late teens and I thought it good for us to spend some time together. There was no snow or ice on the road that night, and we were making good time. Suddenly, we hit a patch of black ice and the truck began to slide sideways. Hitting the guard rail, one of the front tires was torn off the rim and we flipped 360 degrees.

At that very moment, two semis were traveling toward us from the north. They saw the whole thing, stopped, and held back the traffic. I wasn't knocked out, but I lost my hearing aids and broke my glasses. I told Kyle to get out of the car quick, but he couldn't get his door open. Getting myself out of the vehicle, I noticed a small flame under the front wheel. Somehow, Kyle got out just in time. Within minutes, the car was ablaze. Everything was burnt to a crisp - everything that is except my Bible. To this day, I still have that Bible. The edges of the pages are slightly singed, but it's still intact and readable. I thanked God that night, for without a doubt, it was His hand that protected us!

Look at what the Bible says in *Psalm 91:11-12*

"He shall give His angels charge over
you, to keep you in all your ways.
In their hands, they shall bear you up,
Lest you dash your foot against a stone."

The third accident happened in Florida in 2020. While driving down the street in my convertible, I stopped in the left lane to turn, when a man unexpectedly ran a red light. Broadsiding me, the car was pushed all the way across the road to the sidewalk. The car was totaled, but I'm still here, with a mere a scratch to show for it.

"Many are the afflictions of the righteous,
but the LORD delivers him out of them all."
Psalm 34:19

Looking back on all these accidents, I'm convinced we have angels that protect us. There's no question in my mind that they're all around us. Now, why Marjorie wasn't saved from her accident, I don't know. I don't have that answer. Perhaps we all have a moment set in time that is our designated time to leave the earth. Meanwhile, God's angels see to it that our lives are not taken from us prematurely.

Moved with Compassion

At 83 years of age, I have to say I've lived a very full life, and supposedly, God's not done with me yet. One thing I've come to realize is that God puts his fingerprint on everything. Even in our most challenging times, God always manages to show Himself. Take this situation, for example:

Many years ago, I fell off a building which led to three back surgeries. As a result, I have neuropathy in my feet, which causes my legs to go numb.

Not long ago, I saw an advertisement about a new treatment they offer locally, so I looked into it and began a program in January. They gave me seven shots of B12 in each foot. Then they put these cups on my legs for greater circulation to rejuvenate the nerves. Beforehand, a woman came and washed my feet. To my surprise, I began to share the gospel with her.

"Did you know that the last thing Jesus did was wash His disciples' feet?" I asked her. *"It has to be one of the most humbling things a person can do for another person, and here you do it all day long, day after day."* I remarked.

I never would have guessed that I was speaking into the life of someone who was hurting so bad.

That broke the ice, we struck up a conversation, and I listened intently to her story. She had gone through some great difficulties in life, and here she was washing feet. I looked around and noted that some of the feet she washed were covered in sores, red, and swollen. Most people would be afraid to even touch them, but she ministered so gently and graciously, just doing her job. I have to say that my heart was moved with compassion.

I told her, *"If you turn your life over to God, He will give you the desires of your heart."*

Later, I realized the LORD had set me up for a purpose, and I discovered a way to help her out. Actually, it was the LORD who helped her out through me. I was just an instrument He used to minister to someone in need. He does that, you know, and it's a pleasure to partner with Him. It's not something I decide to do. The Holy Spirit initiates it and I'm just a willing vessel, happy to do the LORD's work!

Not long after, I touched base with the woman again, and to my delight, the LORD was already at work. In that short time, she was offered and accepted a promotion that included a significant raise that will meet her needs. What a blessing!

"You're my savior!" she said.

"Oh no!" I responded. *"Christ is your Savior! I'm just an instrument in God's hands."*

> *"And we know that all things work together for good, to those who love God, to those who are called according to His purpose."*
> *Romans 8:28*

An Instrument in God's Hands

My entire life has been a search for truth, freedom, faith, and love, and God has by no means disappointed me. During this time, He has allowed me to experience some things in my life that changed me from what I was to what I am now. Some may think I spend way too much time and resources helping people. I understand that may not be how our world works, but over the years, I've come to discover that it's exactly how God works!

If you can't love somebody here on the earth that you can see, how can you possibly love someone you can't see... like God? *(1 John 4:20)*

People, today, are desperate for the real thing. They want to know real care and real love. In response to that, God releases the fruit of His Spirit, *(Love, Joy, Peace, Patience, Kindness, Goodness, Gentleness, Faithfulness, and Self-Control),* through the actions of His people. Simply put, He partners with people like you and me.

I count it a privilege to be used by Him, and I'm going to fulfill those God-given assignments whether it's popular with others or not. I can't help everyone, but I will extend the love of God to those God asks me to.

When we show people that we care about them and love them, they, in turn, are drawn to God.

Many years ago, there was this one time, in particular, when I just happened to come into some unexpected money. At that same time, several tornadoes pummeled a region not far from where one of my sons was living. Striking hard, many were left in a bad place. It was an awful situation and of course, I lifted them up in prayer. That's when the LORD put it on my heart to take that unexpected money and use it for His glory. In the end, three families benefited and were able to get through that time of devastation a little easier. They didn't know me and I didn't know them, but God knew them. God saw them in their need and provided for them. It's situations like that where people realize God is real!

"A generous person will prosper;
whoever refreshes others will be refreshed."
Proverbs 11:25 NIV

"What can you take with you to heaven? Only other souls."

~ Reuben Beachy, friend

"Grandpa is the most generous person I know!"

~ Celina Jones, granddaughter

"If ever there was a need, Dad was always there and willing to help."

~ Marlin Graber, son

"Martin is a very giving person. He's always sharing what
he has with others. I think Mart's blessings in life
have come from his great heart of giving!"

~ Hank Byler, friend

"Mart has been a blessing to many individuals and
organizations that only God knows and eternity will reveal."

~ Paul Kurtz, friend

"Over the years, I've been inspired by my grandpa's generosity
and love for hospitality. He loves it when people visit, stay, and
vacation at his Florida home. Without hesitation, he welcomes his
children, grandchildren, great-grandchildren, and friends. We all
come and go, enjoying the warm Florida sun and all the fun that
goes along with it. Now that I live in Florida too, my desire is to
carry on Grandpa's gift of hospitality."

~ Dr. Darrin Schwartz, grandson

Remember the Goodness of God

You know, when I started my business, I didn't have nothing... nothing at all! I was so poor that I had to pull spikes out of 2x4s and straighten them up to reuse them, because I didn't have money to buy new ones. For me to come from that, to where I am today, well, let's just say I've never forgotten that. Over the years, the LORD has directed me to do things, half the time without me even realizing it. He provided the opportunities and I just stepped into them. It's got to be that way!

Generosity starts by remembering how good God has been to you. Then you simply allow Him to move through you, in that very same way, to bless others!

It goes way back to my early days when Amos talked me into bringing that small kitchen down to Haiti and installing it in a hospital. I got so much joy from that experience, and it fueled my heart to work with God more often.

"The generous soul will be made rich,
And he who waters will also be watered himself."
Proverbs 11:25

Time Changes Things

You've heard the old expression, *Time Changes Things*. To my delight, I recently ran into an old friend who told me that things are different in many Amish communities these days. Apparently, some of the rules have changed. People are now allowed to own computers, cell phones, and vehicles of all sorts - cars, trucks, and tractors. They even have electricity!

Unfortunately, there's still much confusion - things that don't make sense. An Amish man who now owns his own vehicles hires people to drive those vehicles. The only thing is he hires illegal immigrants. Where's the integrity in that? Another Amish man now owns his own store and restaurant. That's great, but he also has decided to sell liquor.

Sure enough, the Amish seem to be embracing progress, but they still dress Amish, and they still shun people. They still shun me!

Unforgiveness

"If you do not forgive men their trespasses, neither will your Father forgive your trespasses".
Matthew 6:15

Some of my very own relatives can't seem to extend grace and forgiveness to me, even though I no longer own my own business, and they now have businesses that are bigger and far more progressive with technology than what I ever had.

To really make things right, the Amish need to release people like me from the bondage of their shunning.

Some have, but most won't. Before Carol passed away, a neighbor of ours, who just happens to be an Amish minister, stopped by and informed me that he would no longer shun me. I have to admit, that surprised me! It's not something they do. He was having a gathering at his home with a meal and friends, and invited Carol and I to come. To my amazement, they didn't shun us either. I have to say, that was really nice! That's real progress!

Jesus said, *"So in everything, do to others what you would have them do to you, for this sums up the Law and the Prophets."*
Matthew 7:12 NIV

Many refer to this Bible verse as *The Golden Rule*. Now, this a rule that makes sense to me!

I also recently discovered that many of the Amish are installing solar panels for energy. There's nothing wrong with that, but the sad part is that some are secretly wiring in electricity from underneath, because the solar option isn't providing what they need. The solar panels are just a façade, a way of looking Amish. It's that kind of hypocrisy that drove me from the Amish church.

Praise the LORD with Instruments!

On a better note, I discovered that my old church, King Church, now welcomes the use of instruments in their worship. Oh, what joy that brings to my soul! Look at what the very last Psalm, #150, in the Bible declares:

"Praise the LORD! Praise God in His sanctuary. Praise Him in His mighty firmament! Praise Him with the sound of the trumpet. Praise Him with the lute and harp! Praise Him with the timbrel and dance. Praise Him with stringed instruments and flutes. Praise Him with loud cymbals and with clashing cymbals! Let everything that has breath praise the LORD! Praise the LORD!"

Birds of a Feather

To date, I've lived eight decades and then some. With all life's ups and downs, I wouldn't trade any of it, and I've still got some years in me which I intend on living to the fullest!

As I look at my life today, I've come to realize that although I left the Amish Church many years ago, I never really left the Amish community.

**They say, *Birds of a feather flock together,*
and I am definitely a part of the Amish flock!**

You heard me right. We really are all one big quilt of a family and I wouldn't have it any other way! I love the family get-togethers, the dinners, the concerts, the conversations, the building projects, and of course, the ice cream socials! Not to mention, we all seem to be related to one another.

You can't throw the baby out with the bath water!

Everyone is at a different place with God. Where some walk and talk with Him, others disregard His value, and there are a lot that fall somewhere in between. Truth be told, it breaks my heart to see so many wrapped up in religion, yet so far from a personal relationship with God. The eyes of many in the Amish community have been blinded - closed to the fullness of what God offers them. 'Don't misunderstand me. I'm not here to judge. I just want to point people to the door that leads to a full and vibrant life with God.

Jesus said, *"I am the door. If anyone enters by Me, he will be saved, and will go in and out and find pasture."*
John 10:9

A Softened Heart

I will never forget that night in my bedroom when God changed my life! That's where it all started for me, and the process of transformation - making me more and more like Him - continues day, after day, after day.

On many an occasion, I've asked the LORD to soften my own heart. True to His Word, I believe it was on that very night that He took my hardened heart and replaced it with a new one. Look at how the Bible describes it:

"I will give you a new heart and put a new spirit within you; I will take the heart of stone out of your flesh and give you a heart of flesh. I will put My Spirit within you and cause you to walk in My statutes and you will keep my judgments and do them."
Ezekiel 36:26-27

When it comes to the wonders of God, some things are difficult to describe. This book is my mere attempt to present to you my best witness of how GREAT God has been to me, throughout my life.

An Invitation

As I've gotten older, I've become more sensitive. So much so, that when people hurt, I hurt. It doesn't have to be that way, you know. A lot of problems can be solved by simply allowing God to lead one's life.

**The Good News is that God's invitation
is open to all - it's open to YOU!**

*"Behold, I stand at the door and knock. If anyone
hears My voice and opens the door, I will come in
to him and dine with him, and he with Me."
Revelation 3:20*

That's what makes the difference! When God knocked on my heart, I invited Jesus Christ to come into the center of my life, and I allowed His Word, the Bible, to be the Voice that leads and guides me day to day. I found prayer and reading the Bible to not just fill my heart, but to overflow into everything connected to me - my marriage, my family, my business, my associations, into the decisions I make, and the things I say. They are not just words on a page. I have applied them to my life to the best of my ability.

Of course, I am by no means close to perfect, yet I have asked God to shine His Light and His Love through me, to use me in any way He can to make Himself known to others, just as He has made Himself known to me.

So, I ask you, *"Do you know God in a personal way?"* Perhaps God is knocking on your heart? This simple prayer is the first step. Why not take a moment to bow your head and say it now.

~ Prayer of Salvation ~

Father God... I come humbly before You, and I ask you to forgive me for all the things in my life that have not been pleasing to You.

Over the years, I've made mistakes that I'm not proud of. I've said things and done things that were not right, and there were times where I should have said and done things, good things, but didn't. I'm really sorry for that, and I ask You, now, to forgive me.

All this time, I've lived my life my way. I've never really given You a chance - a chance to reveal Yourself to me - a chance to work in my life - a chance to transform me into the fullness of who You created me to be. I'd like to change that! I'm not sure exactly how to do this, but here it goes...

Jesus, I'm inviting You into my heart and life, right now, to lead and guide me, from this day forward. I believe You are the Son of God, and I believe that You died on that cross for my sins. I receive Your love and forgiveness, and I trust that I am now a part of the family of God.

Thank You, LORD, for Your mercy and grace. From this moment forward, I'm turning away from any and all darkness in my life, and I am freely choosing to walk in Your glorious light! Walk with me, LORD! Talk with me! Teach me! Show me how to do this. In Jesus' name I pray... Amen.

"Your Word is a lamp unto my feet
and a light unto my path."
Psalm 119:105

CHAPTER 16

Wisdom

Words of Wisdom Concerning Life

- The most important thing in life is to know and walk with the LORD. With that, you're promised eternal life.

   The fool has said in his heart, "There is no God."
   Psalm 14:1

- Then live your life to the fullest. Enjoy it!

   Jesus said... "I have come that they might have life,
   and that they may have it more abundantly."
   John 10:10

- Sometimes you're in the valley, and sometimes on the mountain top. Praise the LORD during the good times AND the bad. Be thankful for what you have!

   "In everything give thanks for this is
   the will of God in Christ Jesus for you."
   Thessalonians 5:18

- Don't worry! Bring all your concerns to God. He will help you.

   "Be anxious for nothing, but in everything through
   prayer and supplication, with thanksgiving, let your
   requests be known to God, and the peace of God,
   which surpasses all understanding, will guard
   your hearts and minds through Christ Jesus."
   Philippians 4:6,7

- The LORD is Truth. He's the God of the Universe and He's in control. Search the Bible for answers. Seek His face. If you discover your purpose - what it is that God created you for - you'll eliminate a lot of heartache.

"And you will seek Me and find Me,
when you search for Me with all your heart.
I will be found by you, says the LORD..."
Jeremiah 29:13,14

- I made a lot of mistakes over the years, but I learned from them, and to this day, I praise God for His grace and mercy. I don't have anything to say about myself. In German they would say I'm just an *"adaclutz"* meaning I'm made out of clay. Don't let yesterday's mistakes stop you from making good choices today.

"Not that I have already attained or am already
perfected, but I press on, that I may lay hold of that
for which Christ Jesus has also laid hold of me.
Brethren, I do not count myself to have apprehended;
but one thing I do, forgetting those things which are
behind and reaching forward to those things which are
ahead, I press toward the goal for the prize of the
upward call of God in Christ Jesus."
Philippians 3:12-14

Words of Wisdom Concerning Marriage

- I always say, *"Treat your wife like a queen, and she'll treat you like a king."*

- Make it a point to tell your wife, <u>often</u>, that you love her, and do it <u>in front of</u> the kids.

- Marriage is sacred - it's holy and it's blessed! It's one of the greatest blessings we can experience and it's to be treasured. Treasure one another.

- Be an excellent help mate. It's a good thing to have a partner in life - doing things together, the conversations, and praying with and for one another. Make it your goal to be good at that!

- Look to Jesus for advice and do what He tells you. He will help you to be a good spouse, a good friend, a good parent, a good person.

- Granddaughters... Don't ever marry a man who doesn't know the LORD. Trust me when I say that he needs to get that straight first, then get married.

- Don't fuss over the small stuff in life. It's okay if you don't always agree, and you don't have to always be right. Women have a good sense of inner intuition, a sixth sense, whereas men sometimes are quick to react. Consider your spouse's perspective as an asset. They often see things you don't. It's what makes you complete.

Words of Wisdom Concerning Jesus

Jesus is not a religious symbol! He's the One True Living God and He desires to have a vibrant, personal relationship with us. That said, I want to tell you who Jesus is to me today.

- First of all, Jesus is the Son of the Most-High God. He's my All in all. He's pure, without sin. He was sent by God. He's my Joy. The joy of the LORD is my strength!

- Jesus is the Atonement for all my sins. He's a Sanctifier, a Savior, and a Healer. He brings Freedom to live!

- Jesus is the Power that lives in me, and works through me. I'm His representative, His ambassador. It's by the filling of the Holy Spirit that I work in partnership with Him.

- Jesus is the Great Shepherd. He's MY Shepherd, and His grace is sufficient for me.

- Jesus is my Income. People might not think that, but without Him, I don't know where my income would be coming from. He's also my Insurance, my Future, and my Family. I honor Him!

- Jesus is my Fortress, my Shield, my Guardian, my Leader in life. He's my Captain. He's my Physician, my Comforter, my Judge, my Rock, my Strength, my Wisdom, my Everything!

I could go on and on, but that's a good start. What I really want you to know is that these aren't just mere words. Over the years, Jesus has revealed Himself to me personally, in all these ways and more. I can never deny that. My hope is that He will reveal Himself personally to you in ways that you might have your own list.

CHAPTER 17

Tributes

My Tribute to
Marjorie and Carol
My Two Queens

Proverbs 31:10-31

"Who can find a virtuous wife?
For her worth is far above rubies.

The heart of her husband safely trusts her;
So he will have no lack of gain.

She does him good and not evil,
All the days of her life.

She seeks wool and flax,
And willingly works with her hands.

She is like the merchant ships,
She brings her food from afar.

She also rises while it is yet night,
And provides food for her household,
And a portion for her maidservants.

She considers a field and buys it:
From her profits she plants a vineyard.

She girds herself with strength
And strengthens her arms.

She perceives that her merchandise is good,
And her lamp does not go out by night.

She stretches out her hands to the distaff,
And her hand holds the spindle.

She extends her hand to the poor,
Yes, she reaches out her hands to the needy.

She is not afraid of snow for her household,
For all her household is clothed with scarlet.

She makes tapestry for herself;
Her clothing is fine linen and purple.

Her husband is known in the gates,
When he sits among the elders of the land.

She makes linen garments and sells them,
And supplies sashes for the merchants.

Strength and honor are her clothing;
She shall rejoice in time to come.

She opens her mouth with wisdom,
And on her tongue is the law of kindness.

She watches over the ways of her household,
And does not eat the bread of idleness.

Her children rise up and call her blessed;
Her husband also, and he praises her:

"Many daughters have done well,
But you excel them all."

Charm is deceitful and beauty is passing,
But a woman who fears the LORD,
She shall be praised.

Give her of the fruit of her hands,
And let her own works praise her in the gates."

My Tribute to
My Children

Psalm 78:1-8

"Give ear, O my people, to my law;
Incline your ears to the words of my mouth.

I will open my mouth in a parable;
I will utter dark sayings of old,

Which we have heard and known,
And our fathers have told us.

We will not hide them from their children,
Telling to the generations to come the praises of the LORD,
And His strength and His wonderful works that He has done.

For He established a testimony in Jacob,
And appointed a law in Israel,
Which He commanded our fathers,
That they should make them known to their children:
That the generation to come might know them,
The children who would be born,
That they may arise and declare them to their children.

That they may set their hope in God,
And not forget the works of God,
But keep His commandments;

And may not be like their fathers,
A stubborn and rebellious generation,
A generation that did not set its heart aright,
And whose spirit was not faithful to God."

My Tribute to
God

Psalm 71:14-24

"But I will hope continually,
And will praise You yet more and more.
My mouth shall tell of Your righteousness
And Your salvation all the day, For I do not know their limits.

I will go in the strength of the Lord GOD;
I will make mention of Your righteousness, of Yours only.
O God, You have taught me from my youth;
And to this day I declare Your wondrous works.

Now also when I am old and gray-headed,
O God, do not forsake me,
Until I declare Your strength to this generation,
Your power to everyone who is to come.

Also Your righteousness, O God, is very high,
You who have done great things; O God, who is like You?
You, who have shown me great and severe troubles,
Shall revive me again, And bring me up again from the
depths of the earth.

You shall increase my greatness, And comfort me on every side.
Also with the lute I will praise You - And Your faithfulness,
O my God! To You I will sing with the harp, O Holy One of Israel.

My lips shall greatly rejoice when I sing to You.
And my soul, which You have redeemed.
My tongue also shall talk of Your righteousness all the day long;
For they are confounded, For they are brought to shame
Who seek my hurt."

CHAPTER 18

Blessings

The Father's Blessing

"Gather together! ...and he blessed them:
he blessed each one according to his own blessing."
Genesis 49:1,20

~

Wilma, my firstborn...
You have shown and given so much love to your family, along
with our large family. You stood with me first, in the loss of your
mother, brother, and step-sister, and now your step-mother. You
have stood by your husband through much turmoil in the church,
and you are still standing firm and faithful. May God bless you in
the days ahead with good memories. You have learned to accept
situations you could not change, and change the things you could.

"She opens her mouth with wisdom, And on her
her tongue is the law of kindness. Many daughters
have done well, but you excel them all."
Proverbs 31:26, 29

~

Mel...
You have endured many hard things in life, and have overcome
them. Don't forget the things you were taught when you were
growing up. You have been loyal in your constant support to both
me and to *Dutch Made Cabinets.* From your youth to your sixties,
you have learned cabinet making from beginning to end, receiving
many a compliment from both our customers and dealers.

"Let your father and your mother be glad,
And let her who bore you rejoice."
Proverbs 23:25

"For whatever is born of God overcomes the world.
And this is the victory that has overcome the world -
our faith. Who is he who overcomes the world,
but he who believes that Jesus is the Son of God."
1 John 5:4-5

~

Marlin...
When you were a little boy, you took such care of your toys, arranging them all so neatly, and keeping them in excellent condition. That said, it doesn't surprise me that over the years you've made your mark at *Dutch Made,* organizing and shipping parts and pieces throughout the United States, as well as learning the cabinet making business. Well done, son!

"My son, let them not depart from your eyes -
Keep sound wisdom and discretion; So they
will be life to your soul and grace to your neck."

Proverbs 3:21-22

~

Becky...
All these years, dear daughter, you have exhibited precious traits of Loyalty and Endurance. You did a good job when you were laying out cabinet prints, and now you are taking good care of your mother-in-law and children. Life doesn't always make sense, nor do we always have the ability to change things. Never forget that God is always near. He is with you.

"But the path of the just is like the shining sun,
That shines even brighter unto the perfect day."
Proverbs 4:18

Margaret...

You have made a home where your kids and grandkids feel safe and secure. Your thoughtfulness and kindness impact others, more than you know. Oh, how Carol looked forward to the days you came by to clean house for her. You were so good to her. That servant's heart of yours is like gold - a valuable treasure that's hard to find in the world today.

"An excellent wife is the crown of her husband."
Proverbs 12:4

~

Rose...

You are a great caregiver, Rose, always doing something for someone. The grandkids and great-grands always love going to Aunt Rose's. It's because you're a blessing to so many. You're a blessing to me!

"Let not mercy and truth forsake you;
Bind them around your neck,
Write them on the tablet of your heart
And so find favor and high esteem
In the sight of God and man."
Proverbs 3:3-4

~

Marj...

You have many talents. Continue to use them to bless your family and others. You have not fully lived, until you have done something for someone who can never repay you.

"For we are His workmanship, created in
Christ Jesus for good works, which God prepared
beforehand that we should walk in them."
Ephesians 2:10

Marlene...

As a young teenager, your heart was filled with a desire to be a missionary. You went to Russia three times, three years in a row, and it transformed you into a woman with a heart for the lost. It's also what gave you that passion for leading worship.

> *"Go therefore and make disciples of all the nations,*
> *baptizing them in the name of the Father and of the Son*
> *and of the Holy Spirit, teaching them to observe all things*
> *that I have commanded you; and lo, I am with you*
> *always, even to the end of the age."*
> *Matthew 28:19-20*

~

Lynn...

You have had a compassion and desire for music since you were a small boy. I remember when you were taking piano lessons with Dave. You were never satisfied doing your lessons, because they were too easy and boring. You would listen to Marlene playing, and play her lessons too! Use your musical talents, son, for the building of God's Kingdom, praising and glorifying His awesome deeds and power!

> *"O God, my heart is steadfast;*
> *I will sing and give praise,*
> *even with my glory.*
>
> *Awake, lute and harp!*
> *I will praise You, LORD, among the peoples,*
> *And I will sing praises to You among the nations."*
> *Psalm 108:1*

Marty...

You worked so hard for your community as a fireman and first responder. Farming, cabinet building, maintenance... I sent you to a woodworking auction to buy a dust collector and you returned home, moving it by yourself, and completely assembling it. You had so much potential and many things going for you. I wonder, *"What would you say to us today?"*

> *"Now therefore, listen to me, my children.*
> *For blessed are those who keep my ways.*
> *Hear instruction and be wise,*
> *And do not disdain it.*
> *Blessed is the man who listens to me,*
> *Watching daily at my gates,*
> *Waiting at the posts of my doors.*
> *For whoever finds me finds life,*
> *And obtains favor from the LORD;"*
> Proverbs 8:32-35

~

Cami...

Oh, my daughter... You left us way too soon. When I started seeing your mother, you gave us that set of rules and insisted we follow them. I will never forget your laugh and sense of humor. What would you say to us today? I believe you would say...

> *"Turn your eyes upon Jesus.*
> *Look full in His wonderful face,*
> *And the things of earth will grow strangely dim,*
> *In the light of His glory and grace."*

> *"He has shown you, O man, what is good;*
> *And what does the LORD require of you*
> *But to do justly, to love mercy,*
> *and to walk humbly with your God."*
> Micah 6:8

Curtis...

God has given you a Gift of Wisdom and you have already achieved many of your dreams. You've been used in our government's military and other places as well, even being mentioned in the Guinness World Book. May your gifts and inventions be used to make the world a better and safer place to live.

"But seek first the kingdom of God
and His righteousness, and all these
things shall be added to you."
Matthew 6:33

"The fear of the LORD is the beginning of wisdom,
And the knowledge of the Holy One is understanding."

~

Corey...

Back then, you were hurting so much from the loss of your dad. It was easy for me to love you as my own son. I believe that hurt is what makes you want to help children that have been given up for adoption. Your knowledge of the computer has been very helpful in the success of *Dutch Made.*

"Let the word of Christ dwell in you richly in all wisdom,
teaching and admonishing one to another in psalms and
hymns, and spiritual songs, singing with grace in your
hearts to the LORD. And whatever you do in word or
deed, do all in the name of the LORD Jesus, giving
thanks to God the Father through Him."
Colossians 3:16-17

Carlin...

My son, you are special, always helping others and learning as much as you can about farming, *(where my heart still resides)*. You can do anything - like making motors run, no matter what. You have always taken care of me and your mother, dropping everything if need be just to help us. What a blessing you are to those around you!

> *"A good name is to be chosen rather than great riches,*
> *loving favor rather than silver and gold."*
> *Proverbs 22:1*

> *"He who has a generous eye will be blessed,*
> *for he gives of his bread to the poor."*
> *Proverbs 22:9*

> *"The generous soul will be made rich,*
> *And he who waters will also be watered himself."*
> *Provers 11:25*

~

Michael...

Back in the day, knowing the desire of our hearts, God placed you in our hearts and home for ten wonderful years. It saddens me that so much time has separated you from us, because I have always considered you part of our family. Know that our love and prayers for you have never ceased, Michael. Never forget what you were taught in our home as a boy - the story of Jesus - because it's filled with grace and has the power to transform.

> *"You shall love the LORD your God with all your heart,*
> *with all your soul, and with all our strength. And these*
> *words which I command you today shall be in your heart.*
> *You shall teach them diligently to your children, and shall*
> *talk of them when you sit in your house, when you walk by*
> *the way, when you lie down, and when you rise up.*

You shall bind them as a sign on your hand, and they shall be as frontlets between your eyes. You shall write them on the doorposts of your house and on your gates.
Deuteronomy 6:5-9

"But as many as received Him, to them He gave the right to become children of God, to those who believe in His name: who were born, not of blood, nor of the will of the flesh, nor of the will of man, but of God."
John 1:12-13

~

Behold, children are a heritage from the LORD,
The fruit of the womb is a reward
Like arrows in the hand of a warrior,
So are the children of one's youth.
Happy is the man who has his quiver full of them;
Psalm 127:3-5

May the LORD give you increase
more and more - you and your children.
May you be blessed by the LORD,
Who made heaven and earth."
Psalm 115:14-15

The LORD bless you and keep you;
The LORD make His face shine upon
you, and be gracious to you;
The LORD lift up His countenance
upon you and give you peace."
Numbers 6:24-26

A Letter to My Grandchildren

Dearest Grands and Greats,

It's been said, and I have to agree, that there's something extraordinary about the relationship between a grandparent and a grandchild. It's special because it's pure and not overly complicated. We just LOVE one another!

As I sit down to write to you, today, more than anything, I want you to know how special you are to God, to me, to your parents, to your family, and to all those around you. You are precious and your life is significant! No one else is YOU!

You're one-of-a-kind, and God created you with purpose - to love Him, and to love the people around you.

Over the decades, I have visited a lot of places, and I've come to understand something important. The world is so much bigger than our little Amish settlement. Growing up, many people around me believed the Amish way was the only way, but over the years, I've met a lot of people who aren't Amish that know and serve God in the most wonderful way! They walk with Him and they talk with Him.

We are all meant to be personally connected with God.

The sooner you discover who your Creator is, the better. Everything you need to know is in the Bible. Not only that, if you talk to Him, He will talk to you. That's how a relationship with God grows!

I can promise you this... when you find Jesus, you'll love Him.

He really is the friend that sticks closer than a brother, and you can trust Him like no other. It's because of Him, that I have been abundantly blessed in so many ways, that I can't possibly count them all. The list would be so long, there aren't pages enough to write them all down.

Be Free!

I pray that each of you will live in Freedom - free from bondages that will keep you from experiencing the fullness of what God has for you.

Don't get caught up in worldliness. It's fruitless.
Choose God, stay on His path, and you, too, will prosper.

The older I get, the more I realize that I haven't stopped and smelled the roses nearly enough. God's creation is amazing, so be sure to enjoy it! He has created all things for His pleasure, and as children of God, we are meant to enjoy them as well.

There's an old saying and it's true - We come into this world with nothing, and we leave this world with nothing. In my life's search for truth, faith, freedom and love, I have personally discovered that God's way is always best!

Always remember that it's not about the *"things!"*
Things don't really bring happiness, LOVE does.

If you want to experience real love, you need to discover God on a personal level. He is the source of love, and His love is perfect and pure. Once you engage in that yourself, then you can share it with others - your spouse, your children, and all those you come in contact with. I pray you find that love.

It's no secret how I feel about marriage - It's a wonderful
thing! That said, find your soul mate and marry them!

Just make sure you both know Jesus and are serving Him, first.

Each of you has an amazing life ahead of you. Know that my blessing rests upon you. Glorify God in all you do.

With love,
Grandpa

A Final Word

Today, as I look back on my life and count my blessings, I have to start with the fact that I had not one, but two GREAT loves in my life - Marjorie and Carol.

With them, came a wonderful family. In total, there were fourteen children from my marriages to Marjorie and Carol, plus one that was adopted. I can honestly say that I loved each child as my own, and each has blessed me and made me proud in their own special way. In addition, I have fifty-some grandkids in all and thirty-two greats! If that weren't enough, I have more friends than I can number.

For many people, work is a chore, but I loved my work and I loved making cabinets. *Dutch Made Cabinetry* was a gift from God that allowed me to use my artistic talents to touch hundreds of lives in a very practical way.

My music, of course, is what brings joy to my soul. It makes my heart dance! I can't thank God enough for putting in me the desire to learn the guitar, banjo, harmonica and fiddle - even with all the obstacles in my youth that tried to prevent that.

Most of all, I thank God, my Creator, my LORD and Savior, Jesus Christ. From the moment He made Himself known to me, He has walked with me and talked with me, protected me, comforted me, and stayed with me all my days. I owe my life to Him.

If I could leave one most-important piece of advice for those who come after me, I would say this:

Seek the LORD while He may be found."
Isaiah 55:6

I think everything in life happens for a reason. God has those answers. May it be written in Heaven's books for the Graber family...

"As for me and my house, we all serve the LORD."
Joshua 24:15

Over the years, I don't know why the LORD blessed me so abundantly, but it's been a good life, a full life. Of course, there's always challenges along the way, but God is good!

Thank you all for being a part of my story.

With love,

Martin

"His LORD said to him,
'Well done good and faithful servant;
you were faithful over a few things, I will make you
rule over many things. Enter into the joy of your LORD.'"
Matthew 25:23

"Our dad taught us to love the LORD!"

~ Rose Eicher, daughter

"Dad is the salt of the earth, a child of God, a hard
worker, an artist, and a musician, generous, faithful,
steady, and so much more! I'm so proud of who my
dad is and all he has accomplished. I'm grateful for
his love and support throughout my life."

~ Marlene O'Donovan, daughter

"Congrats Martin on a life well-lived
and a legacy well-made!"

~ Curt Graber, son

"He who is faithful in what is least
is faithful also in much..."
Luke 16:10